LOCKDOWN LEGACY

First published 2021 by Network She
www.networkshe.co.uk

Editor: Siân-Elin Flint-Freel

Cover design and book design: Adele Kelly (www.akcreative.co.uk)

ISBN: 978-1-8384050-1-4

CONTENTS

FOREWORD

I t is a year that I, as a doctor, had always worried I would live through but hoped against hope I would avoid. Pandemics have been blighting our world throughout history: during the Plague of Justinian in 541 CE, people were left to die; the Black Death of 1347 led to the invention of quarantine; The Great Plague of London of 1665 saw the sick 'sealed up'. The 19th century cholera pandemic was a huge milestone for public health research: yet despite these advances, the Spanish Flu pandemic of 1918-19 led to about 50 million deaths, a proportion of the world's population equivalent to almost 200 million deaths today.

We have had false alarms during my career – swine flu, bird flu, SARS, MERS. The 'real thing' was inevitable. Yet when it came, the UK was woefully unprepared. We have seen one of the highest death rates in the world and among the largest costs to society.

As a GP, I am all too used to being busy – but even by my standards, the last year has been frenetic. By contrast, all too many of my patients have been without work – furloughed if they were lucky but often falling through the cracks because of zero hours contracts, maternity leave and more. Women and young people have seen their livelihoods and their prospects disproportionately affected.

The last couple of decades have seen the rise of the 'anti-vaxx' brigade, described indirectly by the World Health Organisation as one of the top ten threats to global health in 2019. At the start of the pandemic, I genuinely believed that this global threat would see a damping down of conspiracy theorists – surely everyone would see that vaccination was our way out? How wrong I was. The 'University of Twitter', it seems, has made millions believe they know better than the scientists and the trolling I have received on social media, for trying to put out the fact (no matter how unpopular) has shocked even me.

Equally shocking has been the rise in domestic violence – not exclusively but most commonly inflicted upon women. I have seen a rise in horrifying cases of child abuse, often by parents at the end of their tether. I have comforted wives who have not been able to say goodbye to their husbands or parents before they died, or even attend their funerals.

But among the human tragedies which I have encountered every day have been many rays of hope. The scientific world has come together to develop vaccines – with full safety research – at an unprecedented pace. Overall, as a nation, we have been extraordinarily altruistic, following lockdown rules to protect others. Hundreds of thousands of unsung, unpaid heroes have volunteered to look after the most vulnerable. I hope that when this pandemic finally ends, we will remember these lessons and emerge to a kinder world.

Dr Sarah Jarvis, MBE, FRCG

Clinical Director at 'Patient' and medical broadcaster

INTRODUCTION

Welcome to the *Lockdown Legacy,* where you will find inspirational extracts of an unprecedented time from women of all ages and backgrounds from all corners of the world.

This time capsule ensures that future generations and those too young now to remember in the years ahead have a clear record of how the time of COVID affected each and every one of us, worldwide. We may not have all been in the same boat, but for once the world was sailing into the same storm.

For some, the restrictions of lockdown have been nothing more than a government-imposed inconvenience, but for others it has been a life-changing tragedy, the memory of which will never leave them.

Once over, it will only take a matter of months and this all-consuming pandemic could be a thing of the past, well forgotten. Certain generations will have no memory of it, some generations will choose not to remember it and others will never be allowed to forget.

NETWORK SHE

Exclusively for women who mean business, *Network She* creates opportunities and opens access to a wide range of resources, support services and solution providers via their extensive network of contacts and associates from across the UK and beyond. *Network She* has a growing portfolio of platforms for you to use to share best practice and experiences, gain confidence and develop skills, ensuring you can be the very best you can be.

Nicola Moore and Ruth Lloyd-Williams of *Network She*
going on a post-lockdown road trip

Founded in 2007 by Ruth Lloyd-Williams, in 2021 *Network She* celebrates 14 years of making a difference, creating connections, opening doors and supporting women as they develop themselves and their business.

Network She strives to continue to bring motivation, inspiration, opportunity and fun to the women who mean business. This challenge was achieved throughout lockdown, when face-to-face events were not possible, with the launch of *The Mothership,* a free Facebook Group that has offered support professionally, personally, emotionally and socially to more than 1500 women from across the world.

NETWORK SHE FOUNDATION

All profits from The Lockdown Legacy will be in aid of *The Network She Foundation,* which was founded in August 2015 to support women and young girls into employment, education and sport. The Foundation empowers participation, helping women and girls to thrive and maintain momentum. *The Network She Foundation* will be offering Lockdown Legacy grants for items like sports equipment, personal development courses or to study for a professional qualification.

For more information on the Network She Foundation grant application process, please make sure that you are following the Network She social media platforms where all the details will be posted when applications open:

Facebook facebook.com/NetworkSheOfficial

Twitter twitter.com/networkshe

Instagram instagram.com/network_she/

LinkedIn linkedin.com/company/networkshe

By purchasing this copy, you are helping to nurture the passions of women and continue to support women of the future. You are creating your own Lockdown Legacy – Thank you!

1–Ruth Lloyd-Williams and Carolyn Hodrien heading to the Bradford Bulls' Stadium raising funds and awareness of Kate Hardcastle's IWD Women in Sport Initiative.

2–Empowering Participation. The Mochdre Lionesses Women's Football team taking part in The Fizzy Friday 5K having received funds to support winter pitch fees from The Network She Foundation.

3–Supporting Girls' Grass Roots Football by supplying kit, equipment and a day out at Manchester City where the girls were mascots for the women's team as they played against Arsenal.

4–Raising funds wherever we go to support women and young girls into education, employment and sport.

5&6–The Porth Eirias Runners. A group founded through friendships forged at the Network She Foundation's annual Fizzy Friday 5K, who have gone on to receive funding to support leaders' training, safety kit and equipment.

#RIBBONS4EVIE

All her life, my Evie was a little fighter. She was diagnosed with West Syndrome (a really rare form of epilepsy) as a baby and I was told to prepare for the worst. But Evie had other ideas!

She loved nothing more than having fun with her brothers and sister, going to school with her friends at Ysgol Pen Coch in Flint, and visiting the nurses at Tŷ Gobaith Children's Hospice for respite care.

Evie also loved her clothes and her shoes, she was a real girly girl. I always joked that she wasn't dressed unless she was wearing a bow in her hair. Doctors had said she wouldn't make her tenth birthday, but she proved them wrong and we had a fantastic party with Evie dressed in her tiara and princess gown.

The sign at Tŷ Gobaith was covered in #Ribbons4Evie on the day of the funeral

Before lockdown started, Evie had been in intensive care for six weeks with sepsis and pneumonia, but she was well enough to come home. A fortnight later she had a nosebleed and I thought 'that's not right'. Evie went back into hospital and we were shocked to hear that the sepsis was back.

At the hospital, it was so different. All the staff were in Personal Protective Equipment (PPE) and I had to wear the same to visit Evie. She looked absolutely terrified.

She fought her illness right up until the end, but when they said she was going, I took my mask off and my goggles and said, 'if she is going, she is going looking at my face.'

When she passed away, Evie went to Tŷ Gobaith to stay in their Snowflake Suite. A nurse looked after Evie, just like they had in all the years when she had visited for respite care. Because of the restrictions, only close family were allowed, but I got to spend precious time with Evie and have lots of cuddles.

While we were at Tŷ Gobaith I was thinking about Evie's funeral and what music to have. I was wavering between 'A Whole New World' from *Aladdin* and 'Strong' from *Cinderella*, when 'Strong' started to play. That was Evie choosing!

For Evie's funeral, we were only able to have thirty mourners, which was really sad because in normal times the church would have been packed. As it was, our whole village turned out to line the streets and lots of people came to the crematorium car park.

Tŷ Gobaith started a #Ribbons4Evie virtual event so that everyone could join in and remember Evie on the day of her funeral. Everyone was invited to post a photo of themselves on social media with #Ribbons4Evie and it appeared all over Facebook and the local newspapers. Hundreds of people took part and it was so moving. At Tŷ Gobaith, the entrance sign even wore ribbons too.

The #Ribbons4Evie appeal raised more than £5,000 for Tŷ Gobaith. Evie would have liked that, to know she was helping the other children. It was really touching to know that on 30 March 2020 everyone was thinking about my Evie and sending their love.

Donations can still be made in memory of Evie at
www.tygobaith.org.uk

hope house tŷ gobaith
children's hospices

Linda Davies

Evie's mum

"COVID-19 has undoubtedly changed us."

SPINNING PLATES IN A KITCHEN LOCKDOWN

Rewind to March 2020: two women, two P45's, one double sink, a thousand anxieties and a million dreams!

Having resigned from our positions as Social Work Managers, we were on the cusp of entering a brand-new self-employed world armed only with our values, passion, and plenty of saucepans! The dream was 'Dragon Dinners' – a hot 'Meals on Wheels' service that would cater for the most vulnerable older adults in our area. Our focus was on innovation, affordability, and inclusivity. In a society where you could order anything at any time from anyone, we wanted to stand out and be different. Be personal.

Then the whisper of COVID-19. Like everyone else, we naively believed it wouldn't reach us. Surely it wouldn't be necessary to close restaurants? Limit supermarket trips? Ban us from seeing our families? And then our vocabulary changed. Shielding, social distancing and the R rate suddenly become our norm.

Cue the phone ringing. Ringing off the hook. Overnight our orders doubled, and then tripled. More and more individuals contacted us with concerns about family, friends, neighbours and themselves. We knew we had to respond and respond fast. Our plan to 'build the business slowly' trickled down the kitchen sink as quickly as the many cups of tea we never had a chance to drink.

Two women and their saucepans suddenly became: two teachers, two delivery drivers, two pet sitters, two carers, two personal shoppers, two cleaners, two bakers, two chefs, two post women and two plumbers (yes, the double sink became a permanent feature).

Months whizzed past but we learnt to adapt. Learnt to thrive. Learnt how to spin plates successfully (we had broken many). Most importantly, we learnt about ourselves. That our service was only ever 50% making meals. The other 50% was enshrined in us. Two women. We are our business and we are the service.

In speeding up we also slowed down.

We slowed down to chat to those who were lonely and isolated. Took the time to think of innovative ways to reach people. Our customers affectionately became known as 'Our Lovelies' and our online following grew.

Our plumbing held strong and the support flooded in. Volunteers, grants, gifted donations and keepsakes. Our car boots where never empty and our hearts filled up with pride in all that we were supported to achieve.

Six months later and we are no longer numerically just two women. We have staff, a chef, an office, and a commercial kitchen with a bigger double sink! We have a community that supports us and responds when we call out in need. We are the voice for so many, and still armed with our values, passion, and saucepans, we will continue to build our dream through lockdown and beyond.

COVID-19 has undoubtedly changed us. To the outside world, we are still Two Women. Two Women subject to daily restrictions and constant hand sanitising. But we will forever continue to march forward and expand. Our Business, our families, 'Our Lovelies' and our desire for change remain baked into our very being. Passion, hope, values and dreams embodied within us: Two Women.

Jodie Murphy

Dragon Dinners

ALL THE TEARS

The clouds look down on the plants I've just set;
placed in the ground amidst the pandemic of waiting.

I wait with anticipation for the 'first shoots.'

I wait for the do's and the don'ts that preserve life, or not.

I wait to take my daily walk,
the hour yet undecided, because
I wait while the sun makes its preamble in the sky.

It too, waiting, behind a cloud.

I wait for the computer-generated time slot
for the groceries to be delivered,
And I wait for the 5 o'clock puppet show
with its obfuscation, misdirection and lies.

I wait with bated breath for today's toll;
five hundred, seven hundred, hundreds of thousands
in all the world.

A world that waits as I do.

We wait together, a community across nations, waiting.

We wait in our homes, sheltering from the unknown.

We wait to hold grandchildren, hug parents, kiss siblings.

We wait for children to learn lessons at the kitchen table.

We wait outside windows to wave our love, our worries, our concerns
for old ones, trapped inside virus-ridden homes,
the confused, confused beyond measure.

And we wait while the boffins work desperately to find an answer.

We wait outside hospitals for the loved one who will never reappear.

We wait with bated breath for endangered nurses to survive the unseen,
for doctors to work miracles, and care workers to care unprotected,
uncared for!

We wait in shop queues; at a distance.

We wait patiently in the distanced line for the masked assistant.

We wait to let others pass in the street,
wanting to both shun and hug strangers.

We wait with eyes glistening for news of those
we love,
as all the tears gather.

We wait while all the tears flow;
for the gone,
for the end of waiting.

Mary Hennessey

"My lockdown legacy has been one of loss but mostly of gain."

MEETING MORE THAN
THE UNEXPECTED

M arch 2020 arrived and so did a familiar niggling feeling in the pit of my stomach signalling change. It lay in waiting on the circumference of my consciousness, biding its time, itching to announce itself.

I'd been promoted five months earlier to the most senior position in the only company I've ever worked in, to show me appreciation and affirmation of their utter belief in me from day one and yet, I was restless, anxious, awaiting the arrival of something unknown.

June 30th arrived and as I raised my right hand, fork poised to take another bite of my delicious garlic pasta lunch in that lovely harbourside restaurant in Oslo, my mobile phone rang and I saw my daughter's name on the caller ID, so I made my excuses and answered only for my heart to then drop in dismay.

She delivered the news that her grandfather had passed away. He had lived a good life in Norway and, at 89, had seen so much more than he ever thought he would. I was sad for my daughter. She genuinely loved her grandfather and now, less than three years after losing her father, here she was experiencing a great loss yet again.

As I made my way home from the restaurant, a thought meandered its way into my mind. I suddenly became aware that I had borne this man's last name for twenty-two years (even though I had not been married to his son for eighteen of them) and suddenly inside, I felt the resolute ending of an era.

That very day, I said goodbye to my past and welcomed hello to my future.

Into my life he waltzed, with his brown cocoa skin and curly black hair... oh no wait, that's a CeCe Peniston lyric... my guy doesn't have any hair!

Completely unexpected, but most welcome was he. I've since been navigating the path of transformation from an 'I' to a 'we'. The journey has been exhilarating, scary, fun, confusing – all at the same time. Nevertheless, it's a journey I'd happily take again and hope it'll bloom beautifully like fine wine.

I've learned so much about myself, about my wants/needs/temperament. About the things for which my soul yearned but my mind hadn't quite computed. He gives of himself so selflessly and loves me so boldly, he inspires me to want to be a better calibre human.

My lockdown legacy has been one of loss but mostly of gain. I finally see the sun shining brightly through after many, many years of rain!

Hyacinth Walters-Olsen

"It's OK, they said, it's just for a while..."

WE CAME TOGETHER

T he news came careering into view.
Unwelcome, uninvited and far from
expected.
It's OK, they said, it's just for a while, nothing too
much, for too long, but you too.
Yes you, you too are needed to pull your weight,
comply, do you best, and help see this through.

I don't like this, we aren't ready.
We aren't here to be apart, we aren't made to be
a few, we are made to work together, wherever
and whenever, that's what we do.
It's OK, they said, it's just for a while, nothing too
much, for too long, but you too.

This is awful, it's isolating, people are panicking,
people are turning.
On each other.
That's not what we do.
Where has it come from, this idea of the being
safer when it's just you?
It's OK, they said, it's just for a while, nothing too
much, for too long, but you too.

Look, we are in this for the long haul, you can complain, or you can inspire. It's up to you.
Well is it just me, just me on my own or are there a few?
It's OK, they said, we are here, we can do this for a while, together just us, you join us too.

We can beat this together, we can act it out, pretend you are OK until you are.
That's what we will do.
OK, are you sure, are you with me on this?
It's OK, they said, we are here, we can do this, buckle up, it may be different, but let's take in the new view.
Together, it's not just you.

We aren't on our own, we may be isolated, but we aren't on our own.
We are here, we are all here, it's what we do.
Call us, text us, write, shout.... Whisper. We can hear you; the echo became a crowd.
It's OK, they said, we can hear you, we've got you, it may be different, but we are together.

It's leaving again, careering out of view.
We are here, they said.
You are welcome, invited and always expected.
It's OK, they said. We are with you...

Ruth Wilkinson

The Consult Centre

REINVENTION AND BIRTHDAYS

L ockdown started in utter chaos! We had just moved house. My father, who is 92 and lives with us, had just had a heart attack. He was discharged from hospital early; it being deemed safer to be at home. So, the first weeks were consumed with nursing him and unpacking boxes. I opted not to go out for twelve weeks (to shield Dad) except to walk the dog and to start on the garden. Overnight, my husband was working from home and both teenage children began online schooling. There was a constant stream of meals and washing up!

Lockdown forced reinvention upon me.

As part of a wider charity, I offer cognitive rehabilitation sessions to people who have had a brain injury. My sessions stopped the instant lockdown was announced. Like many others, I was faced with trying to use technology I had never used before. I needed to translate pen and paper exercises to easily emailed documents that clients could access during online sessions. To my surprise, clients began saying it was easier, that they preferred them. I could never have imagined that the sessions would be so popular and would never have made the leap to online without lockdown. This new way of working will remain and, long term, I may well have a blended approach of some face-to-face and some online sessions.

During the first twelve weeks of lockdown, we had seven family birthdays: my father-in-law, brother-in-law, his new wife, my son's 15th, my daughter's 18th, my father's 92nd and my nephew's 7th. As we could not meet, we celebrated with family Zoom calls and improvised cake as flour turned out to be one of the things we could not get for months!

For her 18th, my daughter had planned to go to a cocktail bar. So, in my wisdom (or madness), I decided to create her one at home! The spare 'roof' room was festooned with fairy lights and balloons. I reinvented her old chest of drawers into a cocktail bar. Her bookshelves were stocked with glasses, cocktail shakers and other paraphernalia, a neon flamingo and more fairy lights! It became a great way to distract myself from the daily news of illness and death! We really were in our own little bubble.

On the 22 May, we had my daughter's 18th Cocktail Party. But it was only for us – no other guests were expected or even invited. We FaceTimed my brother in Singapore and, like every birthday of Lockdown 2020, we had a face on an iPad on the table rather than the physical presence of a loved one. My beautiful daughter arrived with sash and tiara and there were screams of joy – a moment to cherish for life. With a Spotify playlist on in the background, Grandad got to enjoy his first ever cocktail to the sounds of Ed Sheeran. Another little moment to cherish!

For me, it was a bitter sweet moment of my little girl becoming a young woman. For my daughter, after weeks of highs and lows of no A-levels, no school, no 'end of school' events, in this moment she could forget it all and enjoy the occasion of becoming an adult. She was a little sad at having no friends over but chatted online until the early hours. All in all, it was a good day!

Lockdown was full of highs and lows, of being challenged in ways one could never have expected. There was, and still is, a nagging sense that life is not quite right. When will we enjoy the freedoms we took for granted?

Alison Burleigh

"I had waited 37 years for this moment."

AN EXTRAORDINARY SUNDAY LUNCH

had been making plans over several weeks to have a special Sunday lunch reunion with family. As plans go, of course, occasionally they fall through, and initially ours was set for earlier in the year. Due to changes in circumstances, we had to re-arrange for it to take place in October, but the precise date was yet to be confirmed. The family were travelling from afar and only had a few days to spare before getting back to their day-to-day routine.

Barely able to contain my excitement, week by week I waited for confirmation of their arrival, hoping that nothing would ruin our plans. Finally, October was upon us and I received word that they had arrived safely at their destination and our arrangements for lunch was set for Sunday the 11th.

I arrived at the venue a little earlier than the time arranged, full of excitement. After about ten minutes, calmness came over me and I composed myself. I wondered how they would react to meeting me. I had no particular thoughts running through my mind of how the day would unfold; I decided to let events develop naturally.

Then I saw them walking across the car park below, and as they neared the staircase leading up to the restaurant, I dashed out to greet them. I had never met the family before, yet a warm familiar feeling came over me and I hastened down the stairs to greet the young man, who by now had taken the lead to greet me with open arms and we embraced each other tightly. I had waited 37 years for this moment, to be reunited with my son. The feeling of a natural bond I experienced between us was undeniably strong.

After he presented me with a beautiful bouquet of flowers, I received a warm embrace from his partner, whilst my two beautiful granddaughters looked on. Finally, we all walked up the stairs and into the restaurant.

The turn of events followed so naturally and comfortably. We talked, we laughed and enjoyed each other's company during the flow of the afternoon. Of course, the afternoon came to an end and it was evident that none of us wanted to leave. However, eventually we had to go our separate ways, but not before promising to meet again as soon as circumstances allowed.

The essence of my story is that my son was brought up with the knowledge that he had been adopted. Unbeknown to either of us, we had both been searching for each other and were finally reunited ten years ago. We have been writing to each other ever since, sharing our life events and simply getting to know each other.

Our Sunday lunch will forever be memorable, as we formed a bond on that day. The future looks positive with an opportunity to start a new chapter in our lives.

Anonymous

Mother

LOCKDOWN REALISATIONS

Lockdown hit me hard from both an emotional and a financial point of view.

My acupuncture clinic was forced to close under the government guidelines, and nine years of building a successful practice was put on hold, seemingly indefinitely.

Forgotten by the Chancellor, who decided that along with so many other limited companies, I was not worthy of any help. No furlough, no grants. Forced to survive on my wits for months on end.

It haunted me especially at night, when I would often find myself wide awake at 3am, mind whirring, unable to see a way out. I worried about my family, about keeping a roof over our heads and food on the table. It made me feel aware that it wasn't just me suffering, but all my patients too. Many of whom relied on their regular treatments to keep pain at bay.

The only option offered was to take on debt. A debt I was unsure I could repay. I decided to use some of my personal savings, putting them into the business so as to keep it afloat. I was fortunate. I refused to give in.

I found another role which helped me bridge the gap financially. It was during lockdown that I had the time to think. It suddenly occurred to me. During the nine years in my private clinic and six years in a hospice environment, I had treated over a thousand ladies going through the menopause with my acupuncture treatments.

The sheer scale of the pandemic and the impact globally made me realise I was thinking too small and that perhaps I could help women across the world by sharing my knowledge with them. 'The Menopausal Godmother – No fairytales just friendly factual help & advice' was born.

With this new revelation, I went back to the beginning, starting my book again. This time writing in the voice of the Menogodmum, not Emma the acupuncturist. As I write this, it is almost finished. I intend to have a full book launch on 1st April 2021, which will be the 5th anniversary of my mastectomy which plunged me into a surgical menopause.

Lockdown gave me the one thing that most writers bemoan – time to think and time to write, and from that has come a whole new perspective.

Knowledge is Power, and my lockdown has enabled me to empower women in the menopause.

Emma Guy

@menogodmum

LOCKDOWN BEFORE THE LOCKDOWN

Summer 2019. I am on a heavenly Greek Island cruise. Returning as I approached my 49th birthday, I was already planning my next holiday.

My husband of seven years and I had a great lifestyle, no baggage: holidays, nights out, city breaks, Sunday afternoon drinking, sleep overs and days out with the grandchildren. I am a CEO of a charity and absolutely love it, have amazing colleagues and have seen much success both personally and as an organisation. Life was so good and spontaneous.

Life is still good; but is it different!

28th November 2020, our grandchildren came to us via a social worker. I was shocked and confused. I won't go into the details as the statutory process isn't yet completed but they were at risk at home following an incident that left the one-year-old with unexplained injuries. Initially we were told it would be a few days, then a few weeks, then 26 weeks minimum and now it's been 38 weeks. We have always done loads with them so we just carried on being the best grandparents we could.

This wasn't enough.

To officially care for our own grandchildren, we had to agree to undergo assessments to be kinship foster carers. Hours with a social worker asking about my entire history, career, childhood, relationships, networks, marriage, finances, and referees asked about my parenting of my daughter.

There were very practical things to sort. Car seat, nappies, clothes, the baby was sleeping in his travel cot in a bathroom. A variety of statutory appointments with little or no notice. Medical appointments for the children, medical assessments for us, a lecture about my weight. I'm not too fat to be an amazing grandma but too fat to be a foster carer.

The first month was school runs, nursery, after school care, appointments, supervising contact, parenting, never-ending laundry, social services assessments. I sobbed nearly every day but did my best to function and make things 'normal' for the children. Luckily, work gave me a month off to sort out whatever was needed.

A month after moving in, it was the older one's birthday, and after spending nearly £240 on a bowling party, gifts and birthday tea at Frankie and Benny's, I wondered if I may have overcompensated slightly. I woke on Christmas eve in a blind panic because, although I had loads of gifts for them, I hadn't organised anything from 'Santa'.

New Year came and I went back to work full time. By now the day time routines kept us busy until 8pm and so conversations with my husband were limited and I was in bed for 9pm.

Did I mention that the youngest wasn't sleeping through?

Thinking of the Easter holiday we had booked to Spain was keeping me sane.

Weekends changed to swimming, cinema trips for Disney rather than Tarantino, the zoo, soft play, McDonald's and the park. We stayed in; it was too hard to get a babysitter due to rules and I was too knackered. The fatter I got the less I felt like socialising anyway. Supermarket shopping with two children became a health hazard. How do people manage?

Success used to be work achievements; now it's getting to work knowing the children are bathed, in clean clothes, the dog is walked, everyone's had breakfast, brushed their teeth, homework's done, and Brownies fees are paid!

I told my husband if he wanted to leave he could. He refused. This wasn't what he signed up for. He says it was; for better or for worse.

My once meticulously tidy house is full of plastic rubbish; odd socks and sweet wrappers. We have gone from being joyous, fun, carefree grandparents to the disciplinarians, care-giving boundary setters, the meanies who say bedtime, brush your teeth, time for homework.

Then the lockdown started... already felt locked down.

Spain was cancelled.

Another 10 weeks at least before we know the authorities' recommendations for the long term future. It's all still temporary and court activity was delayed by COVID.

Every cloud has a silver lining though.

- My grandchildren are safe; happy and thriving.

- I've had an opportunity to bond with my grandson that I wouldn't have had. I was already close to my granddaughter.

- I've learned how to do a French plait.

- The children, whilst demanding, make us laugh every day.

- I've been inundated with offers of moral support.

- My mum (now back in our bubble) has been an absolute rock.

- None of us have had COVID; unlike so many others.

- What I thought I couldn't possibly cope with for 26 weeks has now been 38 and will continue possibly forever. I can do it. We are doing it.

Life is still good; we have settled into a routine (that sadly doesn't include as many porn star martinis as it used to) and for the most part we are a happy family. Lockdown only formalised my sense of isolation and feeling trapped within my own life. Surviving this means we can survive anything. I am not sure about the dog though; he may need some counselling.

Maura Jackson

IT'S OK TO BE IN BUSINESS AND BE INCREDIBLY OVERWHELMED

've been asked a few times to write about what I feel my lockdown legacy is. As someone who is usually never stuck for words, I am this time! It feels like such an enormous task after everything that we've been going through during 2020. It's the year that keeps on giving after all!

So what have I done?

Well, I joined *Network She* back when COVID was something that happened to other people, not us. I was pretty blasé about it if

I am honest. I was so convinced that it would fizzle out before it hit our shores that I never really gave it much thought. Then it hit, and boy did it pack a punch. We went into lockdown and suddenly my worst fears were realised. An extrovert cooped up at home with an introvert husband. I love him dearly, but I need people. I thrive on human contact. Could it get any worse? Oh yes, it's 2020 after all! But more on that later.

Network She became a lifeline. A chance to meet and talk to others. You see, I don't just love meeting people, I want to meet new people! That's really bloody hard when you're stuck at home. So the *Mothership* crew became my tribe. The people that I looked forward to seeing, albeit through a screen. I felt that I'd been given a tiny reprieve.

Lockdown did get worse, just after my birthday; at the end of March I received a call from someone that I'd lost touch with. I was surprised, then shocked, then overwhelmingly sad. One of my friends had died from COVID. It was not the call I expected it to be. I was numb. Lockdown had a new significance to me. It was now all about keeping safe, but at what cost?

Mentally, we've never experienced anything like this in our lives. I have never felt so restless. Do you get that feeling too? You want to do something, but you have no idea what? All of the ideas I'd had for 2020 were thrown out. Boy did that hurt!

My CIC, The Hive Mind Company, was conceived way before lockdown. Plans were afoot to support others with their mental health by becoming a mental health first aid trainer. Well, that went up in smoke! All the plans I had were just falling apart in front of my eyes. But, I am nothing special here. Lots of businesses were going through the same.

I decided that now more than ever I had to share my experiences, in the most honest and authentic way I could. So I started to tell my story. It was raw and honest. The more I talked, the easier it became. The *Mothership* was my saviour and also my platform to share my thoughts.

So what is my legacy?

My legacy is that it's OK to be in business and be incredibly overwhelmed right now. We're doing what we can to keep our ship afloat in what has to be the worst storm ever. That is not what we signed up for!

But if by reaching out, talking and sharing my experiences, makes that storm that little bit easier to navigate, then I am proud for that to be my legacy.

Sarah Steinhöfel

The Hive Mind Company

"The world is starting to wake up again."

THE DAY MY MUM FELL ILL, AND THE WORLD COLLAPSED

The relief was palpable. My brother and I glanced at each other and smiled grimly. We'd set off from Cheshire an hour before and were reaching the highest point of the Pennines on our way to Bradford, where Mum lived on her own. Earlier that evening, after not being able to contact her, we'd called the police and asked them to visit her home. Our brother-in-law had just phoned to say they had broken in; she'd collapsed and was very poorly, but she was alive and the ambulance was on its way.

So began a massive change to our lives. Looking back, it seemed just as Mum had become poorly, the world collapsed in on itself: every stage of the world-wide pandemic has been reflected in our microcosm family life. The world shut down, people hunkering away, separating themselves from each other and the virus. And so Mum's world shrank and my brother and I were drawn into the minute by minute, day to day life of a poorly woman. We shut the front door and focused on her. We shut out the wider world. And the world became her home and her family.

Together, my brother and I have tried to share equally the care of our mother. We made a pact early on that we'd be honest and transparent so that when it was getting too much, when we needed a break, we'd share it with each other. This was not the time for simmering resentment or guilty feelings. But the balance between caring, work and my own family back in Cheshire has been a harder one to sustain. I've found myself trying to smother feelings of sadness that I am not spending the last summer holidays with my 11-year-old before he goes to high school and grows up and grows apart. I find it exhausting trying to work out when I can schedule Zoom calls and remote training sessions in and around care, and all whilst battling Wi-Fi that works intermittently at Mum's home. I miss my husband even as I am grateful for his ability to hold the household together and keep the wheels on the bus.

But this has also been a time for reflection: There are many carers out there, and having been one for 15 weeks now, I have the utmost respect for them. I feel honoured and blessed that I have had the chance to care for Mum. Many others haven't been able to see their parents; some I know have lost their parents to the virus. We laugh and say that Mum is time-served and this is her time to receive the love and care she's unselfishly administered all her life to others. My boys have got to see what family love is about – warts and all, as they say in Bradford. It's not just the birthdays and flowers. It's the carrying upstairs, the washing and toileting, the laundry and cleaning, the laughing, weeping, holding.

The world is starting to wake up again. Mum's operation date is still on hold, but it is there sometime in the future. There'll be a day again, when we'll look back at this period as one where not only did we do our duty but we grew closer: Mum and daughter, Mum and son, brother and sister. And I'd like to think that if Dad is up there in heaven somewhere, he'll say, 'Good on you, you two... and quite right too!'

Catherine Sandland

White Hart Training

LOOK FOR ME

Look for me in the flowers of spring
Look for me in the lambs on the hill
Look for me in the light of the dawn
Look for me in the quiet of the hour.

In the nests of birds you will see me
In the song of the river you will hear me
In the pearl of the shell you will feel me
In the colours of the rainbow you will find me.

Look for me in the peace of the garden
Look for me in your beautiful child
Look for me in your favourite song
Look for me – I am Hope.

Sonia Goulding

Artwork by Elfin Bow

THE ANATOMY OF A WAVE

"A wave's mission is to travel and change the space where it moves, from birth to death."

The first wave hit hard and fast. Though at first a seemingly distant and detached problem thousands of miles away in China, the aftershock from COVID-19 swept across the rest of the world with astonishing and relentless speed. In collective shock and awe, we watched in stunned disbelief at scenes of medical staff struggling to cope with the overwhelming numbers of patients engulfing their hospitals.

Here in Britain, leisure centres and theatres were commandeered and hastily kitted out as emergency field hospitals, and on 23rd March, Boris Johnson took to our television screens to announce a nationwide lockdown. In daily televised briefings over the following days and weeks, behind a banner bearing the legend: 'Stay at Home – Protect the NHS – Save Lives', government ministers, flanked by scientists and medical officers, presented grim statistics of exponentially rising cases and corresponding deaths until, on April 10th, our daily death toll of 980 souls became the highest in Europe.

I became creatively and emotionally crippled. I went from being happy and active within my community, to being terrified and isolated. Too scared to leave the house, I spent my days indoors, crying, bleaching and boil-washing, and my evenings drinking too much. On the plus side, I lost a stone in weight

without even trying – on the minus, I lost my step-mum to the virus on April 30th, just three months short of her 100th birthday.

Yet as spring moved into summer, things slowly started to improve. Cases and deaths began to drop. People were encouraged to go back to work, businesses re-opened, and travel was allowed once more. Rules about meeting up with other people were relaxed, the sun shone, days were long, and people smiled again. For a brief, sweet hiatus, life was better.

Now in autumn, days foreshortened by the long creep of winter shadows, we find ourselves caught in a wave period: the time interval between the crest of one wave and the next. As the rate of the pandemic once again accelerates across Britain and Europe, we are ratcheting at increasing speed towards the peak of a second wave, frightened and unwilling passengers on a grim rollercoaster ride, too scared to look down.

Sonia Goulding

MEMORIES OF THE COVID-19 PANDEMIC

News from abroad crept into our
consciousness.
Death rates soared as we watched and waited.
Denying, in part, the threat of inevitable invasion.
Fear seeped in through the pores
of a trembling society.

Panic-buying essentials:
Toilet roll. Soap. More toilet roll. Flour.
Distance enforced in a sanitised life,
we scrabbled for protection.
A country at war with invisible invader.

Maternal instincts settled with the return of a
son.
We paused. Regrouped.
The five reunited.
Together we faced this insidious intruder.
Prepared for the inevitability
of a country in lockdown.

Two weeks in, and COVID took hold.
All five were infected.
Our gift from hospital worker!

No taste. No smell. Symptoms eclectic.
Uncompromising fatigue and a background
unease,
should worsening take hold.

Gradually we found our way back to health,
aware that others were not so lucky.

Meanwhile, the country rallied.
Acts of kindness, support for the vulnerable.
Clapping in unison for frontline workers:
unsung, underpaid heroes. We thanked you.

Pollution retreated.
Wildlife could breathe.
Some took delight in
a new pace of life.
And questions were asked
about lessons to be learnt.

From the outset I've looked with intrigue
to a country who have chosen
a very different approach.
To live with... not fight.

For this is the long haul,
there is more to come.
With reserves running low,
we'd do well to remind ourselves
to keep compassion on high.

Tamsin Hartley

"You had me at 'pasty'."

ZOOM...
JUST ONE LOOK AND THEN
MY HEART WENT BOOM

t's not every day at work that a complete stranger enthusiastically shouts that they love you in front of a room full of people, unless you are Kylie Minogue – I'm guessing she gets that a lot?

November 2019, those halcyon days where we didn't need to cover our mouths and noses, would give out hugs freely and nobody had heard of the word 'furlough'. Whilst hosting an awards event for local pubs, bars and clubs in Plymouth, my vocal admirer had just collected a prize on behalf of the pub he manages. I laughed and assumed the liquid refreshments had something to do with his show of affection.

A while later, a friend mentioned a mate that was 'just my type' who had seen me at gigs. It turned out to be that same shy man. I was flattered but brushed it off. I was happily single after a difficult time with family bereavement and a history of making terrible choices in men. I was at peace being on my own.

But the universe was not going to let this go and his name came up again in February. Another friend who knew him insisted what a fun and nice fella he is. The old Suzy would have preferred a Nice biscuit rather than a potential suitor described that way, but curiosity (and several gins) led me to send a friend request.

Then we were locked down.

As a comedian, my work stopped abruptly. Thankfully, those more tech savvy organised comedy nights via Zoom and I was grateful for being able to exercise my comedy muscle and perform in front of an audience again – the bonus being I would not have to leave my bedroom and could wear pyjama bottoms (a small mercy as my comedy muscle was not the only thing that could do with a workout!)

Mr Beer Goggles from the awards night had tuned in to watch me perform. He even sent a message to tell me he'd enjoyed the show. Over months of lockdown I watched from afar as he took on creative projects at home and he would show his appreciation of my witty status updates by pressing the 'like' button, the flirt!

As the summer in lockdown crawled by I immersed myself in escapist novels set in picturesque seaside villages, romantic and feel-good. Many people tried dating apps during lockdown, reassured there would be no pressure to meet up, maybe get to know someone slowly. Not for me. I had boxsets to get through and could live vicariously through the characters in *Friends* and my favourite film, *The Holiday*, so no need for any romantic silliness in real life.

At the end of July the day had come, a real-life outdoor comedy show with a real audience... in a park. You'll never guess who had clicked on 'attending'.

Even though I DEFINITELY didn't want any kind of relationship, I made a little more effort with my hair and make-up – just for myself, you know. It felt fantastic having a reason to dress up after months of pyjamas and dressing gowns.

People were overjoyed to be out, interacting and thankful for the return of live entertainment.

Then I saw him, grinning my way as he bought his ticket. I felt a bit coy but 'Stage Suzy' took over. Stage Suzy chatted confidently to the handsome man in the audience, then let real-life Suzy take over and mumble embarrassingly afterwards.

I knew that I liked him, wondered how and if I would see him again. That night I got my answer: 'Hey Suzy, great show. Fancy a pasty?'

We met for a socially distanced steak and stilton (posh!). He was due to visit his family but we arranged to see each other when he got back. We kept in touch with video calls and messages and I enjoyed getting to know him slowly. It cemented that he was one of those 'nice' men that had alluded me for most of my 44 years.

My best friend always said, 'He is out there somewhere, you are just not ready for him yet.' When she met my lovely man for the first time, she looked at me intently and nodded.

In July 2020 the world opened up for a short time and so did my heart. Sorry, made myself feel a bit queasy there.

Thanks to technology and being lucky enough to live in a beautiful city with open spaces and the seaside, we keep in touch through lockdown. Pages and pages of Whatsapp conversations and unplanned video calls. I miss him but count my blessings that we found each other. We plan to travel, to spend long days by the sea and have adventures when the world returns to normal. We'll wait as long as it takes, neither of us are going anywhere (literally).

The secret of finding the right person is the same as the main rule of comedy, it is all about the timing.

William – you had me at 'pasty' X

Suzy Bennett

Comedian

THE CORONA ROLLER-COASTER – WHAT A RIDE!

have never been a fan of rollercoasters. I just don't get them. Ninety seconds of thrills for an afternoon of feeling awful; well, that is my experience of them anyway. I suppose I always knew that we would never be a match made in heaven when I lose my stomach going over a humpback bridge!

When I look back at the excitement of Friday 20th March when Cerys was told no school for a couple of weeks, that's what we all thought. An extra couple of weeks off, happy days. But as weeks turned into months of staying local and key milestones like watching Cerys from a distance leave junior school without the celebrations of a prom, the low points were difficult to deal with. My heart went out to them.

I run my own business and most of my clients are gained from networking. I'm a strong believer in building relationships. So, when all events were cancelled, panic set in. As the main earner in the household and no grants available, the pressure was on. But those relationships have paid dividends and I can't thank everyone enough for their support. The world of Zoom kicked in and work resumed in earnest. The major difference being that the working day now had no official start and end time and usually included a local walk (we've found fabulous places on our doorstep that we had no idea were there).

Then came the homeschooling – Wow!

I'll let you into a secret: when I was in sixth form I nearly went into teaching and always had a bit of regret that I didn't. Well, let me tell you, I'm over it! My social media feeds have been full of parents in the same boat, swapping answers to impossible questions. It's been testing to say the least. However, when we're not arguing, it has brought a mutual respect between Ces and I. She has learnt more about self-employment, tax returns and marketing strategies and I have revisited lowest common denominators, Motte and Bailey castles and African drumbeats!

I think the luckiest part of lockdown was the weather. Let's be honest, with our usual UK summers it could have been a lot worse. A summer we will never forget made the isolation more manageable. Family and friends could visit to sit for a drink in the garden, even if it was difficult not to be able to hug – we are a very huggy family! But that sun could also be a nuisance; I still need to find a way of seeing my laptop screen in the sun – answers on a postcard please.

What have I learnt on this ride? Well firstly, I'm still not keen on rollercoasters! Most significantly, it has helped me deal with why Dad was taken from us in November 2019 – we were able to have those last weeks which so many have missed out on and for that I will be eternally grateful. It has made me appreciate how lucky I have been with the opportunities that have come from these challenges. Through my work I have met the amazing ladies in *The Mothership* and becoming part of the *Network She* team. And finally, and most importantly, there is nothing as important as family. Of course, I knew this, but the memories that we have made as our little household have been unforgettable.

And as the Corona rollercoaster still hasn't stopped, I am just longing for the day where I can meet family and friends and say: "Hug anyone?"

Nicola Moore

MarketMoore & Network She

"The virus has created division between people but it also created a bond."

A MESSAGE OF HOPE

Early morning on the 5th February 2020, I woke up after a restless night and opened the Wechat App to see what was new. I saw a beautiful photo of my hometown Ruian with a big, bold 'LOCKDOWN' across it being shared all over my feed. Thirteen days afterwards, Wuhan had been put in lockdown.

I'd been trying to make sense of the virus for the previous two weeks by watching tons of news and social media posts from China. It was expected but still I was in shock by how quickly it happened.

Ten million thoughts went through my head at that moment:
Who's going to look after my elderly parents?
How long is the lockdown going to last?
Are they safe?
Is there enough food to supply the whole town?

I **CAN'T** fly home to see my parents...
I **CAN'T** get into the town...
I **CAN'T** do anything to help...

I felt utterly helpless and panicked. What now? What next?

I asked myself: if the government can lockdown any town in what feels like lightning speed, what else would they do to contain the virus? The whole situation brought the images of some apocalyptic films to mind. The images and videos I saw on social media didn't help. I felt the PANIC.

I rang my parents on a video call and demanded to hear everything that was happening around them – well, as far as they could see. The next few days were spent contacting my good friends who live nearby to ask them to deliver groceries and frozen food for my parents so they didn't have to take the risk of exposing themselves to the virus. Hours were spent speaking to family and friends as I desperately tried to get a clearer picture of what was really going on and the chances of whether my parents would be infected. I was particular concerned as they are in their late 70s and my Dad has emphysema. So little was known about the virus in those early stages.

The lockdown in Ruian lasted 14 days. A fortnight and the following three months of being restless, concerned and anxious about the safety of my family, my loved ones, Wuhan and the whole country.

In March, when the UK started seeing the increased numbers of infections, it felt like a déjà vu. What had happened in China was repeating itself in my own country. When everyone around me seemed to go about their day as if nothing was happening, I was anxious and helpless because I knew I couldn't change anything. I'm not ashamed to admit that

I took my children out of school a week before the official lockdown announcement. I was totally freaked out with how the government dealt with the whole situation.

The situation was soon turned on its head. My parents started phoning me all the time to check in with us and make sure we were all being sensible and cautious in not putting ourselves at risk. As China's situation improved, in early April, my mum sent me a photo of a bunch of wild flowers she had picked while hill walking with Dad. It was spring. It had been over a month of zero local cases. They finally felt safe to step out and enjoy nature. Dad wrote a poem that day. I felt such a relief and truly blessed that they were well and healthy.

What has happened in the past months has made me realise what truly matters to me. What family means to me. The thought of never seeing them again scared me beyond belief.

I **KNOW** the virus has created division between people but it also created a BOND.
I **KNOW** whatever we are experiencing now will pass.
I **KNOW** we will all look at the world differently.

All for the better.

Yifan Nairn

My Mini Poem:

Roses are red,
Violets are blue,
With the dreaded COVID Lockdown
We are glad we still got you!

Ghazala Jabeen

NORTH WALES BEAUTY LOCKED IN DURING LOCKDOWN 2020

We ended up in a standstill and grateful to be still standing.

The dreaded COVID-19 came knocking on our door after doing its rounds as a 'Silent Killer'.

On 23rd March, here in the United Kingdom, we heard the news that our country was going into lockdown and leaving us feeling a sense of being 'trapped' in our homes. It was like someone turned the lights out. There was a moment of 'What's happening and what do we do now?'

It felt like a kind of a 'war' going on... An unknown battlefield and nobody could come out to fight because they didn't know what to attack and what ammunition to use. The dreaded killer's full characteristics were unknown to the experts, politicians, scientists and health professionals.

We listened to the news of the numbers of deaths going up daily. There was a feeling of being helpless. People couldn't come into the country, and we couldn't get out of the country.

During the main lockdown from March, I was fortunate to have some of the family with me. The children – Charlie, Jennah, Jamie and Lucy – helped get the gardening work done, the house décor improved, thanks to Jennah and Jamie organising it. Family together time was appreciated by everyone taking the time to share household duties like cooking, cleaning, etc.

Although we did miss Mikyle being with us as he couldn't come up, and we even celebrated his birthday in April on a Zoom call. Then Zoom communications went through the roof, from family gatherings to business calls.

I went out nearly every day for my one hour of exercise. I enjoyed sharing my pictures of the everyday scenes of my activities on my social media, as did my friends, and we all showed a lot of care and understanding. I listened to the birds, the bees and watched the butterflies fluttering by. It was a reminder that we have such a beautiful home which we all share, and it's our world.

My daily thoughts as I did my walks:

Some lost lives and some gave birth to new life.
Some lost their businesses whilst others started new ones.
Some found new life, and some found a new way of life.
Some got fit, and others got fat.
Some watched their pennies, and some said their pennies'
worth.
Some lost a sense of hope, whilst others restored faith.
And the theme of 'some' continued...

In the main, the uncertainty became very worrying for all,
including our government. I focused on working on my new
routines and tried to stay aware of the changes.

Ghazala Jabeen

The No1 Marketing Machine

Hedgehog First Aid

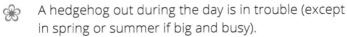 A hedgehog out during the day is in trouble (except in spring or summer if big and busy).

Place in a high-sided box, fill a hot water bottle/plastic bottle with hot tap water, place under or next to the hedgehog and cover with an old towel, bring indoors then call a rescue ASAP. DO NOT FEED.

In the Garden

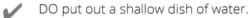

✖ DO NOT feed bread or milk, or mealworms, peanuts, sunflower hearts.

✔ DO put out a shallow dish of water.

✔ DO feed cat/kitten biscuits (supermarket own is fine) and cat meat.

✔ DO leave an area of your garden wild for insects.

✖ DO NOT use pesticides or slug pellets.

✔ DO check before strimming, digging, mowing or lighting a bonfire

✔ Hedgehogs are good swimmers but DO make sure hedgehogs and other wildlife can get out of a pond – provide a shallow area, steps or a hessian sack so they can get out.

✔ DO leave a gap or make a hole (13cm x 13cm) for hedgehogs to move from garden to garden – they can travel up to 2 miles a night.

✔ Keep any netting 22 – 30cm off the ground.

Our iconic hedgehog is now on the red list meaning it is at risk of extinction in the UK

HELPING HEDGEHOGS
IN LOCKDOWN

H edgehuggles Rescue are a not-for-profit trained team covering Anglesey and Gwynedd, helping sick and injured wild hedgehogs.

As part of the team, I have the largest facility so have the greater number of admissions at any time.

At the start of lockdown, we were a team of four, all volunteers working from our homes and we decided to remain open, each of us working solo. I could never have imagined the effect lockdown would have. Initially the year was as expected – releasing over-winterers from our amazing fosterers, though they were released local to their winter lodgings and not where found, as we would usually try to do.

Spring came with the usual orphaned hoglets and poorly adults after hibernation, but as the weather warmed and people took to gardening... My phone started ringing and never stopped. As well as the usual admissions, we were inundated with calls about hedgehogs carrying horrific injuries. It wasn't unusual to have up to seven in a day.

So many people on furlough meant lots of mowing, cutting back and digging, much to the detriment of our little pricklies. Most injuries were from strimmers, one a garden spade, one hedgehog had fallen in a well and sadly, one dog attack. We had an especially tragic week when seven had to be euthanised in two days – heartbreaking and preventable. That was a tough week.

On a happier note, two hogs had surgery by my very supportive vet for their injuries and both recovered and were released.

But the calls just kept coming. At one point, I had 32 in the hogspital. Way above any numbers I had had before. It was almost 24/7 for months.

Normally we would be doing talks and fairs to raise funds, but this year our bank account was being squeezed hard. We did get invited to a 'stay at home' fair, to hold a raffle on Facebook, which was very successful, if stressful. We also did a couple of 'begging' posts for donations.

In spite of lockdown and all restrictions, our fosterers were there when we needed healthy but small patients moved on to make space for the next poorly or injured one. And through the tough times we were there for each other. Now we are a team of six trained volunteers, so whatever comes at us, we will have two extra sites to help save even more hedgehogs needing our help , especially as they are now on the UK's red list.

Sue Timperley

Hedgehuggles Rescue

A time to discover our creativity that is waiting to emerge.

BECOMING A WRITER

For as long as I can remember, I have written rhyming verse. As an excited 3-year-old child, I ascended into fits of giggles over the discovery that saying 'cat, rat and mat' out loud felt special.

I would love to say that I have followed my passion all my life, but the reality is that it's always simmered away on the back burner. Life somehow gets in the way.

Exactly how my story came about is a bit long-winded. Suffice to say that right opportunities/right people/right time synchronised. I have decided to 'become a writer'. In fact, I'll lose the 'become' and boldly state that I AM now a writer.

During lockdown, I have produced my first poetry anthology, 'The Perfect Gift', which is a collection of motivational, humorous, inspirational and spiritual work. It was published in October 2020 under my series 'Sparkle Me Spiritual'. (I have also written Journals, Gratitude Journal/Dream Journal, etc.)

Amanda Anderson

Author

MOTHERING SUNDAY 2020

There is a fixed tradition, that on a certain day,
We all buy gifts and greetings cards, with
meaning to convey.
It is to honour 'mums' (and like), who've nurtured
and supported –
Whose care of us is steadfast and whose love is
never thwarted.
Today though feels quite different – a disruptive
beast's at war
(with humanity, as we know it), it's ripping out
our floor.
Our people are in fear – our infrastructure
swaying,
Our Commerce fractures daily, and our Children
are not playing.
"The best of times, the worst of times" is now for
the Collective –
We're all at risk from COVID threat – it truly ain't
selective!
Our world continues to evolve, great riches
we've attained,
Technology raining from our ears, (a tribute to
'left-brained').
So why (we plea) has this happened? Why have
things got so grim?
What have we done to deserve such blows? Do

the answers lie maybe within?
Our scientists speak complex words as to how
this came about –
Our Medics battle bravely... of this, let be no
doubt.
But what may be the other side? The lessons
we've not learned?
Taken all for granted, abused privilege once
earned.
Are we now being called to stop/re-set, re-think
our errant ways?
Is there light at end of tunnel? Or now close to
"End of Days"?
On this day, we honour those who've helped to
raise us higher,
Let's not forget our Mother Earth, give thanks to
Planet Gaia.

Amanda Anderson

"But still, there is this ache, this hole in my heart where my work used to be."

THE DAY THE CURTAIN FELL

M onday 16th March at 5.50pm, the Adelphi Theatre, The Strand, London. As Assistant Musical Director on *Waitress,* it was my turn to conduct the evening show, but there was a call over the tannoy at 5.45pm to assemble all staff on stage. With a heavy heart, I made my way from the bowels of the theatre where musicians are heard but not usually seen, onto stage, to be greeted by my colleagues.

No one was saying much, there was an atmosphere of sad anticipation of what was about to happen, but even then I couldn't believe the inevitable. The Company Manager, almost in tears, informed everyone that the evening performance would be cancelled and that we should go home and await further information.

I left the theatre, stunned but sure that this would be a short-lived set back. I've worked hard to battle through the competitive world of Musical Theatre, to experience my career goal of opening a new West End show, and I didn't believe it could all end in one evening.

It's been five long months now without performing on a West End stage and I still feel in the early stages of grief. My job is not a hobby, I'm one of the luckiest people who get to do what they love. It's a hard life, it's unstable and financially stressful but the job IS you, it's wrapped up in your identity, and without it I have felt lost, rudderless, drifting in a sea of fear and uncertainty.

Coming to terms with a slower pace of life

There have been some positives: seeing more of my family, albeit online, thanks to matching schedules (working evenings is not conducive to catching up with family with 9-5 jobs); once lockdown was lifted, being able to see friends and family for walks; watching plants in my garden grow from seed which I've never had time to do before, and bonding with my new kitten, Custard, who now follows me everywhere!

But still, there is this ache, this hole in my heart where my work used to be. The likelihood is I will not see inside of a theatre until well into 2021. Producers decided to shut my show, they couldn't afford to keep it open so there is nothing to go back to. It angers me to see people flouting guidelines, not wearing masks, ignoring social distancing and getting back to 'normal'. We are in real danger of losing precious parts of our Artistic Culture. The news is hard to watch, it's hard to see people able to sit next to each other on a plane, or go to the cinema or pub, but yet the theatre is a no-go zone.

But I must remain hopeful, that there is artistic resilience and that we will be back, and this industry that I love will continue to entertain, contribute to the economy and ultimately provide much-needed joy to patrons and staff alike. The curtain will rise once more!

Caroline Grant

"No matter how hard the situation is, there should always be a place for humour."

JUST FOR FUN

No matter how hard the situation is, there should always be a place for humour. And I am sure lockdown is no exception either, though it turned everything upside down.

Well, to be fair, it did not affect my work performance – I am an English-Russian/Russian-English translator at one of the research institutes in Irkutsk – a city in East Siberia – and I was able to get on with my work without interruption.

But I was suffering from the lack of my social life, which usually consists of visiting private viewings of galleries, going to movie premieres, presentations, and parties. These events are very important for me because they provide me with an opportunity to meet friends or get acquainted with people whose interests are similar to mine, and to have an interesting talk with them. These events are worth discussing and writing about , and I even write essays on the city's cultural activities from time to time.

Lockdown completely disrupted this part of my life. Instead, I had to stay within my four walls. It was made more difficult by an unexpected portion of lockdown spare time which provoked me to look for entertainment. I found it in a surprising place – among the scammer messages.

Owing to lockdown, I finally made time to clear my inbox and to get rid of spam emails. But when I looked through some of them, I was amused – I had never really paid attention before – and decided to turn this 'phenomenon' to my advantage. I started to practise my English communication skills online with scammers – the men who search for online acquaintances for financial gain.

If a scammer is a native speaker, you can really use this communication as good language training. I've learned some useful words and phrases for spoken language which were previously unknown to me. Besides, any chat requires immediate responses.

It can help to become quick-witted, especially regarding the extraordinary nature of the situation and the personality of a chat partner, who usually gets nervous when you behave in a way that is contrary to his expectations. The chat gradually becomes heated, thus providing you with a real drive.

The culmination is when the scammer says he would like to come to me – though I never invited anyone to my home – then adds somewhat shyly that he is pressed for money at the moment and asks for a donation. This is high time to use my trump card – the cherry on top: I ask the scammer to whom should I send my money, to him or to a person whose picture he uses as his own. And this is always the end of our 'passionate relationship'.

By the way, it was from scammers that I heard about Google Hangouts. I never used this application before but really like it now! So, even a mangy sheep has some wool.

The older I get, the more I realise the wisdom of proverbs. I've never been so deeply impressed with them before.

Tatyana Leshkevich

"I need a hug!"

ZOOM – FRIEND OR FOE?

Before lockdown was thrust upon us in March this year, who had heard of Zoom? I know my brother had as he uses it daily for work, but me – never heard of it. I do understand a bit about technology, I use it for my lecturing: PowerPoint, Word and Excel spreadsheets, etc. As for anything else – forget it! It's the same when it comes to my car; I know where to put in the key and make it go and where to refuel it. Full Stop. Anything else and I need help. Same with technology. Maybe it's a generational thing, I don't know.

So, Zoom loomed on the horizon in late March.

At the time I was coping with a myriad of issues, suddenly being forced to teach online, missing my students and the dread of hearing my voice on a podcast (more technology). I was dealing with the anniversary of my mum's death and the trauma and stress related to that, along with the inability to share the date or mark the occasion with my father, family and friends. Stress levels were already into the red, but thankfully, I didn't have economic worries to add to the pile of mixed, turbulent emotions.

Then the main focus of my life, the thing that brings real meaning to my life – that too was under threat. As one of Jehovah's Witnesses, my life (prior to lockdown) revolved around being on the ministry, either going door to door or standing at the entrance of a railway station, being outside and meeting people who are interested in learning about the Bible. Gone, along with instructions to 'stay at home' and 'stay safe'. Each week there are two meetings at the Kingdom Hall where we get together as a congregation to encourage each other and learn from God's word. Gone. All gone.

My friends in the congregation are my support network, my listening ear and my cheerleaders, and being with them every day was a blessing. But what now?

And BREATHE.

Because Zoom was looming on the horizon, suddenly we could meet together, if only visually, virtually. I could see everyone; I could be spiritually fed, and I could encourage and be encouraged to stay strong and deal with the chaos of a frighteningly new world where a deadly virus lurked unseen. But it's not the same is it? I miss being with people and isolation is hard.

But you know what? Zoom might be our latest best friend, but it doesn't make up for one thing...

I NEED A HUG!

Jill Bourne

"Then the 'Network She Mothership' became a hive of activity and all us businesswomen turned to support each other."

WHEN THE WORLD NEEDED TOILET PAPER

t was all over the news, everyone was bulk-buying toilet paper. I wondered if the world had gone crazy. It's just a flu or something like SARS, it's not going to be that bad surely...

Fast forward a few weeks and our world was turned upside down. Just at the start of our season, instead of our phone being the hotline to bookings, it was the hotline to nowhere. All bookings were being cancelled and no one was allowed out to play. It all became very real that 2020 certainly was going to be an incredible year, but not for the reason we had hoped.

You see, 2020 was going to be a bumper year.

Our strategy was to be on it with marketing, promotions and doing whatever we could to raise enough to reach our deposit and buy the building where we lived and ran our business. For the first time, I'd even written down what we needed each quarter to achieve our goal and posted it on social media. Then whoosh, just like that, everyone's year was turned upside down.

We wallowed for a bit, not knowing what was going to happen. Were we going to lose our business and home? Gosh, it was terrifying!

Then the *Network She Mothership* became a hive of activity and all us businesswomen turned to support each other: the networking, the ideas, everything. It was amazing and great friendships made that will withstand anything.

I started getting creative, set my sewing machine up to make curtains and blinds for our rooms and posted on social media. Then a group was set up, asking for people to help make scrubs for the National Health Service as Personal Protective Equipment (PPE) was at a shortage. I joined and ended up helping to co-ordinate the 'Scrubs Up Colwyn Bay and Beyond' Team with some wonderful volunteers who remain friends now as I write. Our guesthouse became the hub for collections, donations and storage for all the completed scrubs, masks, hats and bags – the restaurant has often since been referred to as Mike Baldwin's knicker factory!

Throughout all of this, I went live on my Facebook profile every morning while walking my dog, Flash. It has been like sitting round a table having a coffee with my mates; people even say sorry when they have missed me live!

Also, I'll never forget the day I shaved my head for the local zoo, raising £1800 by doing it live on our business page. Hubby got a great kick out of encouraging the donations so he could use the blade to make me totally bald.

My final thought and takeaway from all this: Don't take things for granted, the universe may have other ideas. Be at peace with the reset we have been given.

Tracey Toulmin

Bryn Woodlands House

THE YEAR OF HOMESCHOOLING

From top to bottom: Cianna France (age 9),
Cerys Moore (age 12) and Lyla France (age 6).

MISSING FRIENDS
(AND SCHOOL)

I have been fortunate to have spent lockdown with my family but there have also been a lot of negatives that come with isolation.

For example, when they first announced the lockdown, I was in Year 6, but when we were allowed to go back to school, I went straight to Year 7 in high school. I was very nervous and worried. On top of that, we weren't able to have our year 6 leavers' prom and I was devasted – this wasn't the goodbye I had thought it would be.

Something I really don't like is the homeschooling – not because of Mum's teaching, but I like Mum just being Mum, not teacher. I find it really stressful! Five lessons a day without any interaction with friends and teachers, just listening, reading and writing, is hard going. I never thought I'd say this, but I can't wait to go back to school!

Because we can't go anywhere, it means that I can't see and hang out with my friends, so we now have to do this online, but it's not the same. With the rules changing recently, I got to go for a walk with my best friend. I haven't laughed so much in ages. It was a nice feeling.

Cerys Moore

Age 12

THE BENEFITS OF LOCKDOWN

H ate to be smug about this and, for those that know me, I don't do smug, but I've personally had a fabulous lockdown. Don't get me wrong, my heart goes out to anyone that has suffered, the last thing I want is for anyone to be poorly. But for me, being locked up with my family has been like Christmas without the cake: festering in PJs until lunchtime, developing an enormous COVID belly, not having to tidy the house up before and after guests.

Lockdown has given us all permission to take a step back and make time for perhaps that book we always intended to read, or maybe even write; to brush up on painting skills or take up jogging (not me, of course, that was my husband); being indulgently oblivious to the time of day, or day of the week for that matter.

So far, there's only been the odd niggle. There hasn't been a crossed word yet, but there's still time – looks like there's still another wonderful six months for that!

We've definitely saved on the wallet too. No Friday night parties, so reduced alcohol intake (my liver has gone into a bit of a shock). No nights out means no new clothes purchases, no trips to the hairdressers or expensive taxis home. Also, that claustrophobic mask meant no lipstick or foundation. The mask has put back the double chin surgery for another year with two easy pings behind the ears – simple.

We've all had a little break, a trip to our very own personal stranded island, time to enjoy the things you've always hankered after.

When our children left for London three years ago, I assumed that era was well and truly over, that our job here was done. They were on their own, starting out in life. Never for one minute did I think I'd share another eight glorious months together. I think they've taken ten years off us both.

My son has my husband keeping fit, my daughter still wears my clothes and trashes the place (which I complain about but secretly love). It's a privilege to be able to see and hear them every single day.

I had just managed to recover from my empty nest syndrome, but thanks to this persistent little bug, the nest filled again. No doubt when a vaccine is tested and approved I'll have to endure that process all over again, but for now I'm going to relish every moment.

Christine Allen

"The sense of connection we get from being in the physical presence of others sharing an experience together simply can't be felt through a screen. Fact."

MY LIFE LESSONS IN A GLOBAL PANDEMIC

Today marks our 222nd day living in the 'new normal'. A lot has happened since 16th March 2020, when lockdown officially began...

Restrictions have meant I'm writing this from the same spot my relationship status changed from 'in a relationship' to 'engaged'; the same spot I celebrated turning 30 years old with my family and friends via Zoom; the same spot I logged online for my first day at a new job; the same spot I read an email congratulating me on becoming a homeowner.

I've experienced the highest of highs this year, underneath the darkest of clouds. Woe is me! Not being able to cuddle my mum the day I turned 30 and got engaged. I still haven't been able to hug my nan, five months later. I've only met a tiny percentage of my colleagues in real life, and have no idea when to hand my notice in on our rented property as coronavirus is delaying our completion date. But my mum and nan are just a phone call away. I have a job. I have a home.

If I was to share five life lessons from the global pandemic of 2020, they would be:

⌂ **Gratitude:** On a macro level, Clap for Our Carers brought the nation together and showcased the power of gratitude in helping those on the frontline find the mental strength to do their day job in the most extraordinary circumstances. On a micro level, COVID-19 has shone the brightest of lights on just how fortunate I and the majority of people close to me are, and how we must never take our blessings for granted.

⌂ **Community:** Prior to the pandemic I didn't know my next door neighbour's name, despite living here for a couple of years. I now know all my lovely neighbours – many of whom are high risk – and they know to come to me if they need their shopping doing or a letter posting. We've enjoyed many socially distanced chats, and for the first time London feels like a friendly, safe place.

⌂ **Physical connections:** The sense of connection we get from being in the physical presence of others sharing an experience together simply can't be felt through a screen. Fact.

⌂ **Our planet can recover:** As a direct result of lockdowns across the globe, air pollution levels plummeted, Venice's canals cleared up and animals started reclaiming land. Our planet is loving its detox and if we sustain eco-friendly practices post-quarantine, it will likely recover beyond our imagination.

⌂ **We need less stuff:** This last one ties into the first, because when we count our blessings by hours spent on the phone to loved ones, the ability to lend a helping hand to those in need and the number of toilet rolls in the bathroom, we realise how much we already have... and how little we really need.

Melissa Mackenzie

"My chance to turn a negative into a positive."

TWENTY YEARS A STRANGER

One day your story may become someone else's survival guide.

23rd March – a date in the diary:

- ⌂ My brother's birthday

- ⌂ My sister-in-law's birthday

- ⌂ My wedding anniversary

- ⌂ The day in 2020 that Britain went into a full national lockdown for an unspecified amount of time, in order to try to stop the deadly COVID-19 virus rampaging through the country.

I stared at the final manuscript of my debut novel, *Twenty Years a Stranger*; four years of blood, sweat and tears to get to this point, my chance to turn a negative into a positive. I could hardly believe I had actually done it, written my very own novel, based on the shocking true events that happened to me.

Told through my fictional heroine, Grace King, the story revealed what happened when I received an email out of the blue from an unknown woman, informing me that my husband of twenty years had in fact been living four different lives. I had poured my heart and soul into this and I was confident it was now time to release the fruits of my labour into the big wide world. Unfortunately for me, however, the world had changed forever in the course of the previous few weeks and, in the new order of the pandemic, I wondered sadly whether anyone would notice or care about my book.

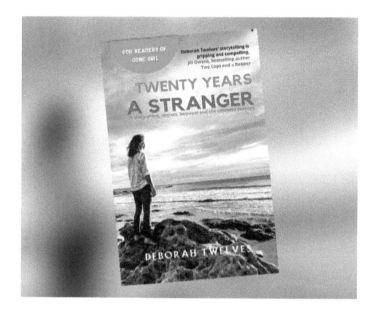

Just two weeks earlier I had been skiing in the French Alps with friends, existing in a kind of alternative reality. We danced on the tables in the packed bar at the foot of the slopes, cheek by jowl with people from hundreds of different locations. Nobody thought of wearing a mask, nobody had any idea of the concept of social distancing. On the way home we heard the announcement that France was going into lockdown in two days' time. Fear of the enormity of what was heading our way began to sink in and it soon became clear we were returning to a very different world, where all our priorities would have to change. None of us could have imagined on that morning of 23rd March just how bad things could get, that we would soon be denied even the simplest pleasure of visiting family.

Of course it was not an ideal time to publish a book, but I had come too far to give up now. Fortunately for me, it seemed people turned to reading as a distraction from the daily worries of the virus and the onslaught from the media about its devastating impact on so many aspects of our lives.

In a world in chaos I reached out to people with my story and the positive reaction was overwhelming. I am happy to think I have touched and maybe even inspired some of those people. Or maybe just given them an escape from reality for a little while. Whatever their reason for reading it, I am grateful and proud that they want to.

Deborah Twelves

Author

PAWS FOR THOUGHT

Thank you to our four-legged friends for their company in lockdown.
Max (Beverley Bradeley), Popcorn (Nicola Moore), Sydney (Caroline
Highman), Dex "Star" (Nicola Butler), Archie (Ruth Wilkinson), Tyson, Charlie
& Snoopy (Claire Evans), Dexter (Michelle Kehoe), Bodhi (Angie Roberts),
Mabel (Jo Mitchellhill) and Gizmo (Elspeth Clark-Ellis)

LOCKDOWN MEMORIES

This picture reminds me of so many things during 2020:

- ⌂ Long hair – no hairdresser for four months.

- ⌂ Lockdown achievement – Couch to 5k – I needed a challenge to keep me focussed during lockdown and followed the BBC Couch to 5k app.

- ⌂ Lockdown achievement – running 5k for charity with a group of other people, all at a social distance. The medal meant so much at the end of nine weeks' training, an amazing feeling.

⌂ During lockdown, I also felt I had become invisible so set up a Facebook group called 'Vicky's Top Tips' which started out as money and energy saving tips and has evolved over the last few months to Top Tips, Throwback memories, fun facts and monthly challenges.

⌂ The picture also reminds me that Teresa and I walked on the promenade at 6.30 every morning – at one stage during lockdown we were only allowed to exercise once a day. It also reminds me to appreciate everything I have and where I live. I can't imagine what it must have been like to live in a city or somewhere with little open space.

During lockdown, I had to learn lots of new skills, including Zoom, social media and building rapport over the phone and Zoom. I've met and become friends with lots of new people, and had great support from many amazing people from all over the country. Distance means nothing now as we don't need to travel; we can conduct business from the comfort of our own homes. But I really can't wait to be able to go out and about, meet people and travel again.

This is a time I will never forget.

Vicky Cutler

Helping you save money on your boring bills

THE SHOW MUST GO ON

n March 2020, I was at school in Plymouth where I am at sixth form studying towards a career in the performing arts. My passion is Musical Theatre and my ultimate dream is to be on the West End stage and to travel the world. I was in rehearsals for a special show to be performed at Plymouth Theatre Royal as part of the Mayflower 400 celebrations. Although I had heard rumours that school may be closed down due to the spread of the virus, I never imagined the extent of the restrictions.

We were told mid-week that school will be closed until Easter from that moment. I remember seeing some older students in tears as they were in the middle of exams. I was thinking it would be nice to have a couple of weeks off school!

In reality, everything stopped.

As well as my A-Levels, in a typical week I attend a Performing Arts Academy, six different dance classes, gymnastics, LAMDA exam classes, private singing lessons, as well as taking driving lessons and working a Saturday job, and of course seeing lots of my friends and spending time with my family. Suddenly I was confined to home and had to do all of these things online. This was very challenging, especially the gymnastics in my small bedroom! The cancelled show we had been rehearsing was entitled 'Some Call It Home'; the irony not lost on me that almost a year later I am still practising my tap dancing in the kitchen!

With A-Levels as well as everything else cancelled, I had to find ways to keep my spirits up. Realising it was important to get fresh air and make the most of the sunshine, I would go out walking, on bike rides and sea swimming in between making funny videos with my friends online. I am very lucky to have access to open spaces and the seaside.

When the restrictions were lifted, as well as feeling free and spending time with the people I had been missing, I also booked an outdoor photoshoot for my dance portfolio. I felt it important to capture myself dancing in a face covering as a symbol of this extraordinary time. I hope one day to show it to younger generations – who hopefully will never have to wear them.

Since October, I have been applying for places at drama schools and universities. I was only able to attend one audition face to face, every other interview has been online.

This week I celebrated my 18th birthday at home with my family and received a steady stream of inventive gifts through the post and some left on the doorstep! Video calls have become the 'new normal' and I felt very grateful to feel so loved. We are now in Lockdown 3 and the novelty of not having to get the bus to school has worn off, but I continue to be optimistic for my future and for the theatres and dance studios to reopen soon, especially as I have worn a pirouette-shaped hole in my bedroom carpet!

I am proud of myself for continuing to follow my dream and look forward to dancing with my friends again... without a screen between us.

Amy Bennett

It was all about the masks.

Photograph supplied by Nicola Combe

THE LOCKDOWN CHALLENGE

During the difficult time of COVID-19 enforced lockdowns, domestic violence saw a disturbing rise in cases, resulting in a sharp rise in child victim displacement.

The Buddy Bag Foundation (BBF) was determined that they had to provide a much-needed supply of Buddy Bags throughout this crisis.

Restoring a sense of safety and security into a child's life during a traumatic time is one of the first steps to recovery. Buddy Bags are something a child can call their own, no matter where they go. Tailored across a wide age range from new born babies to teenagers, they contain all the essential items a child needs straight away, such as toiletries, pyjamas, socks and underwear. They also include comfort items, such as a book, a photo frame and a teddy bear.

Buddy Bags are funded through fundraising, sponsorship and donations. Groups of items can either be donated or sponsored. Individual volunteers or companies usually meet at venues throughout the West Midlands every fortnight to help fill the backpacks.

Postcard from one of the children

Because large groups of volunteers could no longer work together in an enclosed space, the standard way of working was no longer a possibility.

To that end, BBF devised a new way of creating care packages – the 'Challenge Boxes' and the 'Craft Boxes'.

The 'Craft Boxes' contain a selection of materials and equipment to enable mothers and children during lockdown to engage in creative activities together throughout their time in emergency care.

The 'Challenge Box' for businesses is split into two parts. Firstly, team members are tasked with procuring the twelve essential items needed to pack 30 Buddy Bags. Secondly, they are sent the rucksacks to pack. The resulting bags are delivered to women's refuge shelters within the local area.

When launched in January 2021, within a little over two weeks the 'Challenge Box' had already produced well over 900 bags and the programme was growing exponentially.

Enthusiastic knitters produced thousands of knitted toys during lockdown, giving volunteers a sense of purpose during the challenging times.

Also worth mentioning is that over 6,000 Buddy bags were packed and delivered to women's refuge shelters while conforming to strict COVID-19 regulations.

Jessica Phillips MP, Shadow Minister for Domestic Violence and Safeguarding, who is also a patron of the Buddy Bag Foundation, mentioned that an estimated 300 children were temporarily residing in two Birmingham hotels in December 2020. BBF set up an immediate campaign to raise funds. Within days, generous donations were received which enable BBF to pack and deliver 300 Buddy bags and Christmas presents to all these children in time for Christmas.

At a time when most people had had to curtail their activities, Buddy Bags Foundation has risen to the increased challenges and demands and forged forward with a compassion, purpose and enthusiasm that is nothing short of inspiring.

The number of Buddy Bags delivered to children in emergency care has now passed the 30,000 mark.

Karen Williams, OBE

Buddy Bag Foundation

"I missed my friends and family."

MY LIFE IN LOCKDOWN

My name is Ella May Hastings and I am 13 years old. I live in Llandudno with my mum, dad, brother Ethan and my two dogs, Ozzie and Dexter. I used to go to a small primary school called Ysgol Bodafon with my best friend Catrin. I now go to Ysgol y Creuddyn with my other best friend Erin. And this is my life in lockdown!

Lockdown has stopped me doing so many things that I would normally! Such as not being able to go to school, not being able to swim, not being able to see my friends, not go to my grandparents' house after school, not being able to see my sisters, not cuddle my niece and in many other ways as well.

What I miss the most is swimming. I swim for the county club, Swim Conwy. Swimming is my everything. I eat, sleep and breathe it. If I'm not swimming I'm either in school, sleeping or eating. I've made so many friends swimming. It is my hobby and one day I hope I'll be able to say I swam for Swim Wales. I usually swim five times a week and at the moment I have been swimming 0 times a week! I've been swimming since I was three and this is probably the longest time I've not been swimming. Normally when I have to go swimming, I say "Ugh, swimming" and now I'm like:

"When can I go swimming again?"

As I said before, I go to the Welsh-speaking school, Ysgol y Creuddyn. I am in the 'Trochi' form, which means I have extra Welsh classes every week because I am not a fluent Welsh speaker and neither my mum or dad speak Welsh. Going into lockdown has put me at a disadvantage because I'm not getting my six Welsh lessons a week. In Year 8 I might have been going into a mainstream class, but because of lockdown I will have missed about a term and a half of speaking Welsh, which means I will most probably stay in the 'Trochi' form.

I would probably describe lockdown to my children by saying it was probably one of the strangest times the world has ever seen. Also, it's probably up there as one of the scariest times as well. They shut the schools, people stopped working and thousands of people died. It wasn't just Britain that was affected by the coronavirus, the whole world was as well. The country went into lockdown for at least 13 weeks (we don't know how many weeks yet).

My lasting memory of lockdown will probably be that I had at least 13 weeks off school and my mum was being my teacher. We were getting set work on my Chromebook. I missed my friends and family.

In lockdown, I am enjoying spending time with my mum, dad, and Ethan (most of the time). I also enjoy going for walks and bike rides – as long as there are no hills. I also enjoy going on socially distanced walks with my friends. It is sad that we have to stay two metres apart but it's better than not seeing them altogether.

Ella May Hastings

Age 13

SUE PRINCE

Contemporary British Folk Artist

THE BIRTH OF THE NAKED WEATHER LADY

So who on earth would launch a networking events company a couple of weeks before a national lockdown?

Hello, Kat Massey here. Well yes, that would be me! Let me take you on my Lockdown Journey; you really couldn't write it... Oh wait, I am!

2019 and my business partner left our company, Dolittles and Co. It hit me hard. I had to fold the business, I lost all my confidence and was confused on what to do or where to go.

I approached a friend who I had connected with while attending her amazing network events, Sue France, AKA Queen of Connections. I had attended a few of her events and really loved them. I could see that this was lacking in my local area, so I approached Sue for some advice.

Finally, I had a purpose and direction. You know that saying, "2020 will be my year"? Yup, that's the one!

February 27th 2020, I was to hold my first network event. I had sold all the tickets, got three keynote speakers, the hotel, the refreshments, press and TV coverage. Despite being nervous at first, as soon as it started I felt I was home, watching the guests absorb the knowledge, interact and make new connections. This was my calling.

Then Boris said to stay at home...

Not another business that was going to have to close! But yes, exactly that. We were devastated, to say the least. All our businesses closed overnight. What were we going to do now?

Sit on a pity pot and not get dressed is what I did. Then I woke up. It was happening to the world, not just me. How could I help people? I had a Facebook group of around 200 people set up in February for the events, so I thought, 'Why don't I help people to show up, be visible and get dressed?'

Sounds basic, but it's exactly what I did. My challenge week, 'Let's get dressed to de-stress', was a huge hit and it was helping people. I loved it! OK, what else could I do to help them and their businesses show up and be visible? I knew my mindset wasn't great and I knew we needed some fun, so I introduced The Naked Weather Lady.

We had a heatwave. I kept showing up online in just a bikini or boob tube, but when you go Live on Facebook it cuts some of you off, so I basically looked naked! I didn't care. It was bringing joy to others as I read my tongue-in-cheek news broadcasts and asked Alexa to say our Daily Affirmations.

We came together as a community, exactly when we needed it the most. My work continues to help people (and therefore their businesses) show up as them, authentically and to know 'You are Enough', you always have been. Even in a world crisis, together stronger, until we meet again.

Kat Massey

Visibility Queen and Naked Weather Lady

"2020, on paper, was going to be my most successful year."

I SURVIVED AND MY
BUSINESS SURVIVED

I am a busy mum of four young children (all under nine),
a military veteran of 26 years and owner of Mummy and
Theo's Little Baby Boutique. My lockdown legacy will be the
fact that like most others, I survived and my business survived!

In fact, I had another business, KJ's Entertainments Ltd, a children's soft play equipment hire company that also did inflatables and candy carts, etc. I founded this company five years previously, in 2015.

2020, on paper, was going to be my most successful year and I was mostly booked out between March and September 2020 and beyond.

The pandemic hit the UK in March 2020 with a lockdown. Over a 48-hour period, I lost 95% of my bookings for 2020. Unfortunately, I was unable to claim any government assistance to keep afloat because as a company director, I would have taken dividends from the business, and coupled with a military pension, meant that I didn't qualify or receive any sort of compensation.

What next?

Well in April 2020, I pulled on those big girl pants and got a job at a COVID-19 Testing Centre in Llandudno as a Traffic Management Operative, directing and assisting members of the public in the administration of a self-test before marshalling them off site again. Three weeks after starting, I was promoted into a supervisory role managing 26 operatives. Clearly, someone saw my worth (even if I didn't). I subsequently took several courses in traffic management and became qualified to work on roads and construction sites.

In November 2020, the company asked if I would be interested in a Site Manager role. Heck yes, I'd be delighted to move up in positions, even if that meant an hour commute to Liverpool each way and each day. Two promotions in a year, just what I needed to keep my confidence up and food in the mouths of my children.

I am now a Site Manager at a COVID-19 Asymptomatic Test Centre in Speke, Liverpool. I love my job and now manage a team of over 50 employees. All of this whilst caring for my children, who luckily have remained in school, and running Mummy and Theo's Little Baby Boutique.

Mummy and Theo's was born after two of my children were born prematurely at 28 weeks and 35 weeks respectively. With both babies, I experienced difficulty with finding clothes to fit. There are an estimated 60,000 babies born prematurely in the UK every year, yet in both a local and national search, there was almost nothing out there. The clothing range caters for babies from 1.5lbs up to 10lbs, from sleepsuits, dresses, trouser and top sets, to a selection of accessories.

I don't know what will happen next as at time of writing we are several months into 2021 and are still amidst the pandemic but, if you happen to see me on the A55 working – beep your horn and give me a wave!

Korena James

Mummy and Theo's Little Baby Boutique

"People need support more than ever."

THE 'GIFT' OF TIME 'STOOD STILL'

ocked down and living in a cottage on the mountain seemed like a blessing compared to most. The luxury of mountain views, sunshine and my two crazy Springer Spaniels for company was not something I felt I could or should complain about.

What was once full days of clients popping in and out soon became incredibly quiet and very still – almost an eerie silence.

The initial few weeks, I made the most of the 'time off'. Although, I soon realised I missed not having a purpose. My beautiful therapy room became my 'go to' space for my reading and reflection.

A 'gift' of time, I thought as I continued to review my workshops and website whilst attending numerous Zoom training sessions. Not once did I believe I would see the fall of my business as a possibility. I was simply 'on pause' and excitedly filled my days manifesting my visions.

Along came opportunities within The Mothership – the Network She Facebook group which took me completely out of my comfort zone. At the same time, this thrilled and motivated me to have a role during the lockdown.

From this newfound confidence, I opened a Facebook group for my business and began to offer clients help and support with a series of live talks and videos. Something I would never have had the nerve to do pre-lockdown. This gave me back my purpose and I began to offer distance healing for free to support the NHS and key workers during this surreal time.

I found myself holding interviews with my clients on Zoom for my Facebook group and for the *Network She* group. The Mothership interviews became a regular weekly spot and I looked forward to meeting so many inspirational women and sharing their stories to help and support women in business.

My son was granted army leave, and I was so pleased to have him home. The lockdown had certainly highlighted how important well-being and family is. Unfortunately, in early June my dad had a major heart attack and had to have urgent heart surgery. Not being able to see him was so difficult for all of us, especially my mum. His recovery has been slow, but we are so blessed he is still with us.

As the restrictions lifted, it was so lovely to be able to see friends and family and to begin to see my clients returning. I was so excited to open the Crystal Cabin and be able to support people with their well-being once more.

A few months later, my family are in local lockdowns and the same looms for Wales. After the excitement of being free again, we face the disappointment of cancelled events, and a loss of business once more.

People need support more than ever, so for the next few months I shall be taking my business online. 2020 isn't over yet! There's work to do to step into 2021, ready to take back the time that stood still.

Michelle Louise

Angelic Healing

"You're on mute!"

A TOUCH OF TECH ANXIETY

W hen I was a child I suffered from what we now know to be Maths anxiety. I used to get so worked up before my maths lessons, thinking I wouldn't understand, that this affected my performance in class and I didn't understand! Luckily for me I attended a progressive school in the 60s which followed the same blueprint as Gordonstoun, the Scottish boarding school that Prince Charles attended, and allowed us to give up lessons we didn't like for subjects we excelled at, so from the age of 14 I had double art instead of double maths.

This problem continued into my chosen career as a dress designer. I hated pattern making at college and grading (making your original pattern fit different sizes) brought me out in a cold sweat. Anything with a technical side had me flummoxed. I was lucky, my boyfriend at the time was good at these skills so I married him!

I had a successful career in fashion which involved always delegating the technical issues, and then in my 60s moved into running women's networking events. I absolutely loved holding events and helping women connect face to face. And as to the finance side, well the man I met after my divorce when I was 40 was an accountant so I had married him!

Then came lockdown, and with over 800 members of my group to support, I had to face technology, but even worse, I was now 71! After a lifetime of avoiding techy things, I had to learn in order to help others continue to connect and grow their businesses.

Since March 2020 I have done regular Facebook Lives, created a YouTube channel and even mastered Streamyard. I have taught my 96-year-old mother to Facetime on her iPad and I can talk her through when she gets into difficulties. However, I just can't master Zoom. Whenever I join one and I see someone I know, I want to go over and give them a hug and have a chat. They just make me sad.

At last a glimmer of hope.

As lockdown eases I can see my grandchildren again. The nine-year-old is teaching me TikTok and she has created a series for me where I give tips. This has become an instant hit, and although she is raising the pocket money stakes, hopefully this can continue. I won a competition too. The six-year-old has given me a Roblox character and today it came first in a Fashionista vote with her guidance. So I have come full circle; I am designing again and delegating the hard bits!!!

A big bouquet of flowers has just arrived at my house from someone who has found a full time job through my connections. And yesterday I received a big thank you from a lady who has been making thousands of shields for the NHS. She needed a charity manager and I found her one.

Who needs Zoom?

Sue France

Creative Connecting in Cheshire

SHIELDING

#LymphomaLass

I'm surviving Hodgkin's lymphoma. I'm in remission (Phew!) but I understand that the cancer has caused a permanent deficiency in my cell-based immunity to infections. There's no guarantee a vaccine will work for me, so I'll have to wait for everyone else to have theirs before I emerge....

Hi! My name's **Lymphoma Lass** and I'm shielding pretty strictly at home... just going to life-or-death medical appointments (so I went for my annual flu jab, but not to routine non-urgent dental appointments) ...and I go for an occasional walk when no one's about...

I had Bleomycin in my chemotherapy and that helped save my life, but is toxic to lungs ...and I've got a rare type of pneumonia hiding dormant in them too.... It attacked when I was in chemo and nearly killed me... so I know how tough a stay in *Critical Care* is for patients....!

I've also lost my spleen (a major part of the immune system) and now have to take penicillin twice a day for the rest of my life, not eating or drinking anything except water each time for 3 hours to help make it work. ... I had SANT (Sclerosing Angiomatoid Nodular Transformation). There were only around 130 recorded cases of this tumour type worldwide before mine (most found at autopsy), so no one knows what that's done to my immune system....!

I'm a freelance creative now, and since lockdown I've been selling my art on Redbubble, a web based print-on-demand service. Obviously, I'm missing opportunities as an artist and other nice things too. But I believe all the things I miss now will come back one day ...and I can wait. My priority is staying well and alive, for those I love, so as not to cause them the pain of loss and bereavement. I'm working on making the most of each day I'm given. That's quite enough to do for now.

P.S. I crocheted my cape and pigtail wig for a laugh while in chemo, but the satin gloves are serious PPE. Not everyone washes their hands and I've not got back up and walking from the 5 broken vertebrae chemo gave me to lose it all to a little stomach bug... or Covid-19, for that matter.

Lymphoma Lass

"I drew this picture of me and my mum in lockdown as my happiest memory."

Ava-Grace Needham, aged 9

THE UPS AND THE DOWNS
OF LOCKDOWN

As a psychotherapist, hypnotherapist and mindset coach, much of my work involves helping people deal with mental health issues including anxiety, negative thinking, and stress. Clients normally visit my therapy room at home in Altrincham but when lockdown began, all my appointments had to be cancelled. I continued to offer Zoom appointments but most clients either didn't feel comfortable working online or didn't have the privacy at home to be able to talk confidentially.

There was a lull while people waited patiently for the situation to end, thinking it would all be over within a few months. I decided to use this time positively by creating an online course based on my book *Your Flight to Happiness: A 7-Step Journey to Emotional Freedom*, something I'd been planning for a while. When time went on and there was still no light at the end of the tunnel, clients who really needed help started booking online sessions and business began to pick up.

Under normal circumstances, I enjoy attending women's networking group events near where I live, but of course they all had to be cancelled too. However, organisers soon began to offer online events in their private Facebook groups and I was asked by one group leader to present Facebook 'Lives', teaching group members how to change their thinking, release anxiety, feel calm and manage stress. Initially it was daunting, never having done a 'Live' before, but I discovered to my surprise that I actually enjoyed my experience.

I was soon invited to speak in other online groups and during one such experience, I made a connection with an inspirational woman who's based in the USA. She introduced me to a TV company producer in Miami, who after interviewing me on her show about my book and my work, invited me to become the show's Transatlantic Media Correspondent. This involves inviting interesting and inspirational female guests to appear on the show and share their stories. I'll also be in front of the cameras, presenting alongside the regular presenters; all very exciting and has come about as a result of the changes imposed during lockdown.

Knowing how badly COVID–19 has affected the health and livelihood of so many people, I feel very fortunate that the only negative effects I've experienced as a result of the restrictions are being unable to see my family. I was particularly disappointed that we had to cancel the special birthday celebrations we'd planned this year for three 'turn of the decade' birthdays. My mother, who lives in Liverpool, turned 90 in March and my daughter Melissa, who lives in London, turned 30 in May. That day became even more special when her boyfriend proposed to her on the morning of her birthday, after asking my permission the day before!

It was great that we were able to connect via Zoom, although not the same as celebrating in person.

Apart from my son who lives with me, I've only seen my family members once over the past eight months and I am particularly missing my daughter very much. As I write, Christmas is exactly two months away and right now nobody knows whether we'll even be able to meet up in person then, or for my own 'turn of the decade' birthday which is 7 days before Christmas. Meanwhile, I practise what I preach and remain positive, taking things one day at a time and refusing to go into the 'what-ifs' which lead to anxiety and stress. Just hoping that it won't be too long before things get better...

Toni Mackenzie

Inner Depths

"THE EVERYDAY LOSS OF HELLOS AND GOODBYES"

THE EVERYDAY LOSS

The permeating undercurrent
   of deep unease
The questioning flow of
When or if ever lurking
beneath the surface
most times

The loss born alone without
End or ceremony
Or suitable acknowledgement
The loss of a parent and best friend
Landscape changing
any time

Business, so much more than
Just business
This journey into other people's lives
And hearts and futures
Made evermore powerful
At this time

The everyday loss
of a structure
Never really knew I needed

now without it
finding ways to
Manage time

The everyday loss
Of hellos and goodbyes
Lost routines and love
holes widening without end
questions and doubts
fearing time

Chris Kent

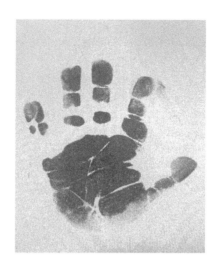

MYLO GEORGE

T he restrictions of COVID lockdown began as nothing more than a government-imposed inconvenience for us as a family.

2020 was a year full of celebration. We would celebrate our 30th wedding anniversary, my father's 90th birthday, my husband's 60th birthday and the birth of our second grandson. 2020 was a year full of milestones which we had planned to celebrate as a family on a cruise around the Mediterranean.

On the 7th of April 2020, the government-imposed inconvenience turned into our life-changing tragedy. A day we will never forget. This was the day the COVID pandemic forced my daughter at 39 plus weeks to hear the words that her son had died, he had no heartbeat. She was all alone, with her partner forced to wait outside in the car park.

Because of COVID, my youngest child had to hear these painful words alone, without the comfort of her partner or family. Because of COVID, my daughter then had to break this harrowing news to her partner over the phone, that their son had passed away. We will never recover from the horrors my daughter faced alone that day!

Lovely Mylo George, you were delivered on the 8th of April 2020; our gorgeous, perfect grandson weighing 8 pounds 8 ounces, with mops of black curls, and you melted our hearts.

 Proud grandparents we will always be. We will cherish the hour we got to spend with you, to hold you, cuddle you and weep over losing you.

I'll never forget the surreal day when we were ushered onto the ward to meet you in our masks and gowns. The fear of contracting COVID was nothing compared to the pain of losing you and the pain of knowing I couldn't make your mummy and daddy feel better.

Your mummy and daddy got to spend time with you in the hospital as a family. They cuddled you, bathed you, loved you and I know they didn't want to leave you.

Sadly, on the 30th of April 2020, you were laid to rest. Because of COVID restrictions, only immediate family were allowed to attend. Your mummy and daddy asked everyone who wanted to remember you to light a candle. We were overwhelmed by the love shown by family and friends.

So little perfect Mylo George, I made you a teddy bear. A teddy bear which gave me comfort, knowing he was with you as you were laid to rest. Your big brother has one for him too, to love and cuddle. It was this teddy bear that inspired me to make bears to bring comfort to others who have lost loved ones too. So as a legacy to you, little man, I have named the bears 'Mylo's Bears'.

We think about you every day and grieve that we will never get to hear you laugh or giggle, or see your little toes wiggle. There are many things we will never get to do, but the hardest thing is not being with you.

We have planted forget-me-nots which will flower every year on your birthday. It is these flowers that inspired me to call my new venture 'Forget-Me-Knot by Wendy'.

We will never forget you, Mylo George xx

Wendy Stoneley

Mylo George's Grandmother

FOOTPRINTS IN THE SAND

"As hard as lockdown was, getting to spend time with my daughter and granddaughter was amazing. Although made bitttersweet as all I really wanted to do was hug them."

Teresa Carnall

(with her daughter, Anime Samah, and granddaughter, Carys)

THE LOCKDOWN SNAKE

How did a steel heart frame holding 100 plus stones decorated by all ages of the local community start? Boredom!

It was back when we could have our one daily outing for exercise and I remember I used to push my luck and drive to the next town in desperate need of change. I always drove with a pack of toilet roll on my passenger seat in case the police stopped me so I could pretend my mum needed the toilet roll...

On one of our walks, we saw a stone snake in Penrhyn Bay. We loved going back to see it as each time it was getting bigger and bigger. In particular, it was the 'all ages' of creativity we liked seeing, as well as spotting the ones my boys put there.

One day I asked my boys whether we should start one of our own. At that time, they'd pretty much say yes to everything I suggested, and I'd exhausted all the obvious: PE with Joe, den building, baking, drawing, and bubble painting (we ended up with a trip to A&E after my youngest drank it rather than blew it through the straw!!!). We even grated a bar of soap with food colouring and put the pieces in an ice tray to make bath crayons one day!!

Each day I balanced work from home, Zoom meetings with the background echo of "Mum, is my bum clean?", homeschooling and keeping a home. I admit some of my ideas for an activity were getting ridiculous – I think wrapping porridge oats and lavender in cloth for the bath was up there with the bath crayons! Painting stones brought me back down a peg or two...or four!!

So one day, that's exactly what we did. I drew up a poster to tie to the park railings, the boys put five or so stones down to start it (including ones we had decorated for our fairy gardens – see, I really didn't miss a trick), and I messaged my friends... admittedly it was more of a demand they get a stone there ASAP. And then after that, I couldn't face the park for a good week as I was too nervous for the boys in case it was a complete shambles.

It really was quite the opposite. The original stone snake had some amazing art! And week by week it got bigger. The journey thereafter to what it is now was absolutely lovely, meeting new people, and my boys loved seeing its development.

I've really laughed at some of the things I've done in lockdown and at 'that mum' I became on Instagram, parading "look what we've done", but the stone heart in our local park is a forever keepsake and we love it!

Did I say we did a keepsake book in lockdown and it made the last page?

Rachael Pierce Jones

Snake Charmer

"I'd been afraid to tell friends how I was feeling."

THE DISASTER I DIDN'T SEE COMING

Lockdown? That'll be easy, I thought to myself. I live on my own. I work for myself, from home. Everything will be just the same as normal. And for the first few weeks, that's just how it seemed, especially with the glorious weather on side.

What I didn't notice was what I can only describe as a heavy feeling creeping up on me. Not all the time. Rather, it came in waves; sometimes I felt fine, others, I felt really low. As the days went by, feeling low became more frequent. I tried to make sense of what was happening.

It started with a description. The colour was dark grey like clouds before a storm. The feeling was oppressive, also like a storm brewing.

It took a bit longer before I found an explanation for my misery. My friends. I love my friends and they are very special to me. Lockdown had taken them away from me. I felt so alone. How I wished I had a dog to be my friend. The gloom was compounded by everything being closed. Normally, I go out a lot. I try to squeeze in some healthy behaviour and go swimming a few times a week. I'm also a frequent visitor to theatres, museums, galleries, cinemas, concert halls, coffee shops, bars and restaurants. Sometimes alone, but more often with friends. All these places were now closed and my friends far away.

I couldn't imagine how things could get any worse and kept plugging away at walking 10,000 steps a day, photographing beautiful spring flowers and trying to work.

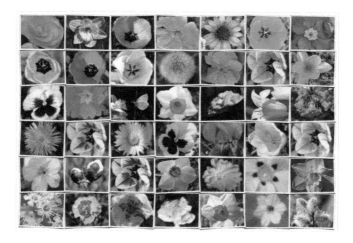

Every day, I went to the cemetery, which felt less busy and safer than the local park. It was far easier to socially distance there. It wasn't long, however, before they closed the cemetery and I was forced to walk in the park, a place where I felt particularly vulnerable as runners pounded towards me, inches away. Social distancing? Hah!

I tried reaching out to a few people I know slightly in the local area, but they seemed to have their own things going on and I felt as if I was intruding. One day, walking through the park, the freshly-mown grass masking the pitfall ahead, my foot hit a hole in the ground and I fell, severely twisting anything that could be twisted! The pain was excruciating. Somehow I staggered home. I decided it wasn't broken and did the RICE thing – rest, ice, compression, elevation. A friend brought crutches and I was housebound.

I felt worse and worse and it all culminated in a meeting when I simply broke down and just sobbed my heart out.

By the end of that dreadfully low day, I decided to take the next few days off. No computer. No social media. No feeling guilty about not working. Just be kind to me. Everyone in the meeting was so kind and checked in on me over the next few days and weeks. That weekend, I started a jigsaw puzzle – a fun depiction of key landmarks around the world. It helped me tap into all the lovely memories of happier times, living and working in so many of these countries. I binge-watched The Crown and generally chilled.

I reached out to my immediate neighbours and told them "I have never been so sad and lonely in my entire life. Can we please do something together?" They came to my rescue. That same evening, we had a socially-distanced barbeque in the garden. My spirits soared.

I'd been afraid to tell friends how I was feeling. I didn't want to be a burden, so I tended to put on a brave face. Now I decided to tell them how much I was struggling. How stupid of me not to confide in them earlier. Life changed that day. We're all there for each other. We're all sharing. Sometimes we listen, sometimes we help and sometimes we ask for help. We often have a glass of wine or a refreshing G&T, play bingo and complete puzzles; we're even writing a story, taking turns to add the next paragraph or two.

One thing is certain, I'm so lucky to have the most wonderful friends in my life and I can't wait for the day we can be together again.

Lyn Roseaman

Now You're Talking

BUSINESS AS UNUSUAL

A fter weeks of watching the coronavirus take lives across the world, on 30 January 2020 the World Health Organisation declared the COVID outbreak a Public Health Emergency of International Concern. On 11 March 2020 it was upgraded to a pandemic. On 23 March 2020 the British government put the UK into lockdown.

We were to stay home and stay safe. We had no idea what the next few weeks would look and feel like. Or that those few weeks were going to stretch into months. We would all celebrate at least one lockdown birthday and life would feel very different – in fact, 2020 was a year like no other. It felt very different to different people, even people from within the same family.

For Ethan Hastings, it was the best time ever – he got to spend every day at home with his Mum. Ethan is 9.

For Ella Hastings, it was a nightmare – she got to spend every day stuck at home with her little brother, Ethan. Ella is 13.

For Rhian Hastings, it was a balancing act – she had to close both her businesses, homeschool her children, Ella and Ethan, and try her best to hold her family together, keeping a roof over their heads and food on the table whilst doing daily workouts with Joe Wicks.

For Paul Williams, it was business as usual – he still got up early every day and went to work. Paul is a postman. No mask, no hand sanitiser, no social distancing. Paul is Ella and Ethan's Grumps.

For me, Ruth Lloyd-Williams, it was business as unusual.

Network She had just launched *The Mothership*. A closed, private Facebook group, that as an addition to the *Network She* portfolio, offered a safe place for women to ask the questions they needed and wanted to ask away from the glare of social media. It was anticipated, when launched in February 2020, that this new 'safe place' would grow slowly and organically.

Then COVID kicked in. Within weeks, the crew of *The Mothership* grew and grew as women reached out for help, support and a feeling of normality. The *Network She Mothership* is currently made up of over 1500 women from across the world.

While flour became gold dust and loo roll was almost currency, *The Mothership* offered a place of calm stability as well as access to help, support and resources. Ensuring that even through such unpredictable times, *Network She* was still able to support women professionally, personally, emotionally and socially.

For me, Ruth Lloyd-Williams, wife and mother, lockdown was a time of separation and loss. A time of birthdays missed. My mother-in-law's 100th birthday celebration was tea for three. Happy Birthday, Olive! As was her 101st birthday in March 2021.

There were no sleepovers at Grandma's house or kisses and cuddles. Any interaction was through a closed window as the grandchildren grew up without me. No Sunday fun days with a big roast dinner, football banter and a game or two of Tangalooma – the rules of which nobody understands.

Holidays were cancelled and the big trip to Australia to see my son, Joss, who we have not hugged since we waved him off on his travels in August 2018, is still a year away.

At the time of writing, the lockdown restrictions in the UK are starting to lift. Children are back at school, everyone has had a haircut, businesses are opening their doors and getting back to the new normal. Yet there is still turmoil elsewhere as people die in the streets, oxygen supplies are spent and the international media reports state there are a total of 16.5 million cases of COVID in India.

In other news, the British media are asking "who paid for Boris' apartment makeover?"

First world problems – Business as Usual.

Ruth Lloyd-Williams

Founder of Network She and Captain of The Mothership

"Then the world turned upside down."

MY KATIE

New Year's Eve 2019, it's 4am at a dark, wet Manchester Airport and I am saying goodbye to Katie, who has been with us for ten glorious days but is now returning to Italy, where she has lived for five years. Her move was an adjustment, but we soon got into a routine, building to five visits a year, me to her, her to me, quality over quantity became our thing.

Had I known on that wet New Year's Eve morning what has now come to pass I would have hugged her that little bit longer... or ripped up her passport and bundled her back in the car! We thought we had just three short months to wait until my first 2020 visit and our week of good food, fine wine and more memory making.

Then the world turned upside down.

Roll forward 10 months; so much has happened that we have not physically shared and my heart aches for that loss. We have Skype and FaceTime but they do not allow us to reach out for a supportive cuddle or a reassuring hug. There have been promotions, births, birthdays, deaths, a complicated surgery, a 30th wedding anniversary, a house move, all of which would previously have involved get-togethers, gatherings or celebrations. There have been none.

It is a year where my 'excitement' amounted to a long walk or a haircut.

It is a year I need to forget but also never will.

It is a year that has distanced us physically, psychologically and socially, a year that we will never get back.

It is our 'lost year', my darling daughter, and may 2021 bring us all better fortune.

Ruth Ballantine

WE ARE STRONGER
TOGETHER

I t's been nearly a year, and
things seem to be the same.
Nothing's getting better, nothing's
really changed.
I feel that awful sadness, the one
we all know well,
missing friends and family, their laugh,

their touch, their smell.
Is this our new normal?
Is this our new forever?
I feel it's never ending, are we
stuck like this forever?
I'm sick of these four walls, from
the house I used to love.
It feels more like a prison now,
but we must rise above.
Homeschooling gets me down, the mum guilt
is rife.
But these children need structure,
stability and a life.
We try our best, we crack a smile,
and we are pushed to the limit.
Then we run a bath, climb in and
cry for just a minute.

Be Kind, Reach Out.
We are stronger together.

Lauren Smith

BEING A TRAVEL AGENT
IN 2020

A s I sit here and try to think of how on earth I can sum up what it's like to be a travel agent in 2020, I am actually laughing to myself. If anyone could see me now they would wonder what on earth I was doing – laughing as I type furiously on the keys of my overworked and tired old laptop! I think it could be hysteria?!

Perhaps I will talk about how I have become completely OBSESSED with checking my emails every five minutes, waiting for the next load of cancellations or flight amendments to come through. Or perhaps I could talk about how many of my clients are now on their 2nd/3rd and even 4th attempt at amending their holidays. Or how about the fact that not many travel agents have earned any money since March, but have had to work harder and longer than normal hours to get refunds back for their clients or to re-work complicated itineraries for next year.

Maybe I could write about refunds – did you know that I have managed to get refunds for all my clients who were due to travel March/April /May /June/ July and August – except one – MY OWN BOOKINGS?! Yes, that's right, just me left to get her refund.

Now it is October 2020, and the Canaries have just opened to us Brits – Hurray! We have taken new bookings this week. I had to refresh my brain on how to load a new booking on our system, it has been that long. Then came the announcement today that the Canaries will be asking for negative tests to be done at the traveller's expense... Oh that will be a joyful conversation...

Many of my travel friends are considering leaving travel or have left now. Some have taken on part time jobs to see them through the winter. It's devastating to think how many good people we will lose. The airport staff, the travel agents, reps, transfer drivers, entertainment staff... the list is endless. It even extends into catteries/dog boarding kennels – if people don't go away, they don't need Fido or Pussy to be looked after!

I don't mean this to be only a negative piece.

I AM enjoying more time with my daughter. I'm enjoying the comfort in knowing that when this is over, people will be wanting a holiday. I know it will be busy again. I know that for those businesses who looked after their clients throughout this, they will be remembered and hopefully rewarded in the long term. One thing is certain; people need hope and something to look forward to – travel ticks both those boxes.

Till we fly freely again...

Rachael Quinton

Quinton Travel

"You have tested positive for COVID."

"Remember to socially distance."

"Hands-Face-Space."

"You've got to self-isolate."

YEAH, WE MADE IT...
WAIT...WHAT?

February 2020, life is calm – as calm as life can get with two highly spirited boys aged seven and five. Me and my husband are both serving police officers, working shifts, a whiteboard to organise the family. We are content. I have just written my first book. A book all about focusing on the positives in life. Called *Look for the effin rainbows*. Oh, the irony!

March 2020 – Lockdown happens. It's OK, we've got this, we have a whiteboard. As my job is more office based, I opt for working at home and homeschooling. I always thought I would be a good teacher so now's my chance. How hard can it be?

We have a timetable, snack money, Lego sets and a trampoline. What more do we need?

The timetable goes out the window, literally, on day two when I have my first meltdown. Their snack money lasts till first break and they are now on the trampoline counting to one hundred (maths – done).

Day three, I give them the Lego sets (problem solving – done). What I didn't realise was I would have to sit with them to find each miniscule piece of Lego for the next two hours.

In the first three days I have addressed five work emails – and when I say addressed, I mean opened.

Day four, meltdown number two for me. I lock myself in my bedroom and try and calm down, doing thirty minutes of meditation. Mum guilt kicks in. I go downstairs to start again and the little darlings have barricaded the front room door.

We carry on in a similar vein until September.

On 1st September, my husband and I skip out of the school grounds, high fiving each other, a quick Dick Van Dyke click of the heels. The boys return to school unscathed and relatively sane. I can't say the same for us.

The boys adapt to their new routines of washing hands and getting their temperature taken daily. Life regains its calmness.

We did it! Wait. What's that?

You have tested positive for COVID.

Not just me, my husband as well, just to test our resilience that little more. Once again, the four of us have to self-isolate.

Self-isolation when we were fully fit was hard enough but when we are both ill, with two boys full of energy, it is a whole new level. Amazon takes another battering, with parcels to occupy them arriving daily. They spend the majority of the time naked, looking like feral kids, while my husband and I take turns to sleep. I say take turns but to be honest, there were times we overlapped, and the kids made themselves lunch of spreadable chocolate on cheese slices.

Day nine and we're nearly there. My husband and I are still on speaking terms, the kids are healthy, and to be honest, they are the only positives I can find but they are pretty big ones.

So here we are, nearing the end of our COVID nightmare. But are we?

Irene Wignall

"This is my chance to build something better this time."

AN ARTIST'S LOCKDOWN LEGACY

I am an artist who looks to nature as a source of creating colourful abstract art.

I usually have dedicated time for painting and administration during the week and weekends. However, in March 2020 this ALL changed in the form of the first lockdown – limited time in the business, homeschooling and juggling part-time work commitments as an Operations Manager in a university.

My business model had been predominantly mural design, which was growing in traction. I had five projects which involved murals with interior designers in the planning. However, other options were taken in light of the pandemic. I knew early on that I needed to change and took some time to redirect my business. After initial analysis of 'first contact to delivery' for murals and commissioned paintings, it was clear to me that paintings were by far where the quickest turnaround and margins were. I started online marketing training for artists and gained two artist mentors during this time. As well as being a member of *Network She*, this has helped me gain resilience in the business. It was a time of growth in the way the business was evolving but not quite connecting as well on the creative level, due to the lack of time or snatched time. With artists, I have come to realise it is all about the mindset and if you cannot achieve the mindset, little else will follow!

The first lockdown for me had a sense of freeness to it; we were in spring and there was warmth and colour and a sense of everyone taking stock. I created a few pieces, but these two stand out for me in my lockdown legacy.

⌂ **The Carnival of the New** – The emergence of summer in this strange time.

⌂ **Too Close to Home** – The separation from family, knowing that the peninsula of Llandudno and mountains were a protector, of sorts.

The latest lockdowns have been more introspective for me due to the lack of time creating. However, my thought process and research into the way I want to continue as an artist has been invaluable.

I have a new collection for sale in spring 2021 on the theme of 'Connections' which explores a time in my life and who was in my life at that time. Some people are still here, and others sadly are not. The collection forms a story about their influence on my life told through art.

⌂ **Growing up** – Connections Series spring 2021– connections through early teenage, friends had a huge impact on my sense of worth.

⌂ **Open** – Connections Series spring 2021 – looking at the start of university, connections and the world comes to life!

I feel that my work has evolved and taken a new direction and for that I can only be grateful for this enforced time of reflection.

Angie Roberts

Angie Roberts Art

"Keep Calm and Keep Your Mask On."

DOING MY BIT

Being over 70 (71 and 3 days on the day this photo was taken!), I was considered elderly and vulnerable. And although I don't consider myself either of these things, it was a huge relief to be invited for vaccination. Not only that, but I felt by having the vaccine I was doing my bit, I was helping us all get out of this dreadful period in our history.

The label on my coat? This was the time I could leave after waiting 15 minutes to ensure I was OK after my jab. I am so grateful for the amazing work carried out by scientists to get the vaccine to us so quickly.

Ann Girling

THE SHOW MUST GO ON

Myfanwy Twankey

WHAT HAVE YOU GAINED FROM LOCKDOWN?

R ecently I was asked the question, "What have you gained from lockdown?" and my answer, in true panto style, was weight! We all had a giggle about it, but it got me thinking about what I have actually gained from the past 10 months.

To say I am a busy person for most of the year is an understatement! A look at my diary for the week prior to all this craziness shows a week full of teaching, rehearsing, auditions, production meetings... the list is endless. But it all stopped and overnight my diary was wiped clean, at first for a few weeks but then for longer and longer.

Obviously, it's totally understandable why it all happened, but it's heartbreaking when you have spent so much time working on things. For instance, I was in the final week of rehearsals for a youth production of *Hairspray*. (Bet you can't guess which part I was playing!) We had spent months in rehearsals and we were days from moving into the theatre to start our tech and dress rehearsals and then performances. Of course, it wasn't just me it affected; we had a cast of at least 35 children and you can imagine how they felt, plus all the unseen help that you don't see when watching a show – for every person onstage, there's at least two more behind the scenes!

Also, that week I had my first rehearsal for a show I was choreographing that was going to take place in June. Again, even though it was a first rehearsal, the preparation time that had already gone into the show was amazing – productions, meetings, auditions, casting, choreographing... Well, the cast smashed their first rehearsal and were on fire and raring to go, but that was the last time we all got together and saw each other.

Panto is a major part of my life and when we finish one season, planning pretty much starts on the next one. Positivity reigned and plans were still going ahead throughout lockdown until... this year's show got postponed, as did most.

So where does that leave us now? Months into it all and the arts continue to suffer and struggle to survive. I am definitely one of the lucky ones as I have received help and support from various sources, but there are plenty who haven't. It's soul destroying to see very talented friends, performers, musicians, artists and technicians not able to survive and having to take on additional jobs or change careers to make ends meet.

I guess that's the way things are and there is nothing I can do to change the situation. You have to keep smiling and carry on with things. Over lockdown I've tried to do this with videos and classes to keep people going. It's made me realise how much the arts mean to people and what effect it has on each and every one of us. So perhaps that's my lockdown legacy – some videos that have made people smile, and we have needed that smile for sure!

I have learned how much time I spend working on various things and how little downtime I allowed myself, but then that's the thing, when you're self-employed, you have to take the work when it is there. Also, I've learned how much we all value the social aspect of our lives and how we interact with each other – seeing friends on Zoom is good but it really doesn't beat that in person connection you have when you are in the same room.

The good news is that things are slowly starting to change with all aspects of life. Change is good. As always, we adapt and move with it. Within the arts, companies are looking at how productions can go ahead and what needs to be done to make it all secure. Indeed, I consider myself very fortunate as I am going to be working over the Christmas season as the Lion in *Wizard of Oz*. It's all these little green shoots that we need to nurture to help ensure the arts are able to continue and bring what we need in life from them. There is a famous theatrical saying that "the show must go on", and if I have anything to do with it, it most certainly will!

Rob Stevens

a.k.a Myfanwy Twankey

*"Seeing someone in full PPE
was quite a shock."*

DODGY DEALINGS

L ittle did I realise that a brief conversation over Twitter
would lead to one of the strangest experiences (despite
COVID) I would have in 2020.

We were two months into lockdown, people had already been
fighting over toilet roll, there was a shortage in pasta, and
everyone had become a baker – flour was like gold dust and
Mary Berry was getting concerned.

The other scarce item was hand sanitiser. You could not get
it anywhere; shelves were emptied within seconds of a new
delivery. On eBay, you could pick up a small bottle for about
£10. It was crazy!

On the 4th May 2020, I was scanning Twitter, not really up to
much and generally enjoying the lovely weather, when I came
across a tweet. A company was offering small bottles of hand

sanitiser for £3.50 plus postage. After a little bit of online stalking, I discovered that the company was legit, and even better, local. I couldn't believe it!

After a brief exchange of messages, the deal was done – cash exchange for two bottles (for Mum and my brother). To avoid the postage, we agreed to meet in Llanrwst on 5th May 2020 at 1pm.

At this point in lockdown, I had only been out once in two months to go shopping and we were in a five-mile rule, so couldn't travel any further than that unless it was essential. To be fair, where I live, I had to travel over five miles to get to a shop, but still felt a little apprehensive as this was about eight miles away – but this was essential and I would only be out for a short while and could do my shopping whilst there.

Before I left for my epic hour out, I washed the money (yes, this is completely true) and placed it into a sealed plastic bag.

It was lovely driving that day, the sun was out (again) and for a second, everything felt normal. When I got to Llanrwst Co-op car park for 12.50pm, there was no sign, but then again, I hadn't asked him what he looked like. He only said that he would be there after the food delivery at 1pm. So I messaged him. No answer. Rather than waste time, I went shopping, bought some treats, nothing that would make a decent meal.

By this time, it was gone 1pm – well, choosing the right wine took a bit of time, you can't rush those things. So I called him again. This time he answered and said he was standing opposite the entrance by the bins. I looked over my shoulder and there was a guy in head to foot PPE. He was wearing a blue boiler suit, a face visor, face mask and gloves. At this stage, this COVID was all very new and no one was wearing face masks as such, and seeing someone in full PPE was quite a shock! He looked like a spaceman or the chap out of Breaking Bad.

Feeling slightly anxious and not sure if someone was filming this for a prank, I walked over. We stood two metres apart (this was even before the rule came out – yep, trendsetters, it was our fault). I said hello and started to build up to a big conversation. Well, I hadn't spoken to anyone in days, happens when you live on your own – had even started to call my gathering dust kettlebell Wilson and regularly said, "Good morning, wall."

He mumbled something, which cut me short, and nodded to the post next to him. Instinctively, I placed my bag with my bleached coins on one post, explaining that I had washed everything and the bag was sealed. He placed his plastic bag containing the two bottles on the other post. I grabbed it quickly and popped it into my pocket, whilst he did the same with the coins.

Anyone watching, well they could have thought all sorts. I tried to carry on talking, but he was not in a chatty mood and left. The switch was done and the deal a success ...everyone walked away unscathed, albeit feeling a little strange to what had just happened.

Never in my life have I felt so anxious about buying two bottles of hand sanitiser. The strangest of days!

Tansy Rogerson

"I felt an overwhelming responsibility to protect them."

I COULDN'T SIT BACK

A s the COVID-19 pandemic spread, I could see first-hand the impact it was having on key workers. Some were dying and it wrenched my heart as our daughter is a community nurse. I'd formed close links with the NHS as a former police sergeant and I'm so proud of our NHS. I couldn't sit back.

I had been building my art business and had taken the huge step of building a workshop and buying a Laser Cutting and Engraving machine. Whilst wracking my brains as to how I could help, I realised that this technology could be utilised to make PPE medical face shields.

After researching design options for reusable hygienic shields, I selected a design with a polypropylene headband and acetate visor, sourced the materials, and adapted my laser machine to cut them.

Soon I was producing 300 visors daily, helped by my husband, Bill, and my sons, Scott and Sam. The next step was to set up a funding page, Shields4Cheshire&Merseyside, to pay for the materials and distribution, and then to appeal for discounted materials from manufacturers.

Senior clinical nurse Rachel Bilsbury receiving 4,000 face shields at Merseycare NHS Trust.

Desperate requests for PPE flooded into the Facebook page from NHS and healthcare workers. The University of Chester Energy Centre Technical Team helped double production. The Centre had been closed, yet they re-opened to help. Also, the shield's design underwent successful substance control trials at Stepping Hill Hospital, Manchester.

Then something remarkable happened. Following an appeal for help on Facebook, a small army of dedicated volunteers joined the campaign. Some friends, some complete strangers. The team phoned every hospice and care home across Cheshire and Merseyside to establish exact needs and match to available production.

The GoFundMe page raised £5,500, which allowed the visors to be donated. We were overwhelmed by people's generosity and kindness, and moved to tears often. It was an incredibly emotional experience, all the little boats pulling together across the country.

As demand spiralled, the need for more capacity became apparent as we grafted from early morning to late into the evening. The amazing generosity of Kath Doran at Spectrum Plastics meant production rose to 10,000 visors per day as everyone working from 6.30am daily, 7 days a week.

In just five weeks from start-up, Shields4Cheshire&Merseyside supplied 18,000 visors to the NHS, front-line health workers, not-for-profit across Cheshire and Merseyside, North West Ambulance, Community and Mental Health Trusts, hospitals, GP surgeries, homeless workers, care homes, hospices and carers. At time of writing, the small Shields4 network has delivered over 200,000 visors, mainly across the North West of England.

What spurs us on is knowing what a huge difference it makes to protecting our frontline NHS and key workers whilst they save lives. Nurses and carers have been emotional, even tearful, and so relieved when receiving the shields, and I felt an overwhelming responsibility to protect them.

The project has even reached impoverished areas of New Mexico, including the Tewa Native Indian women on reservations. My heart burst when I received a wonderful letter of thanks from them.

It was an extraordinary time I will never forget.

Tracey Telford

A PATCHWORK OF PERSONAS

Writing this lockdown legacy has been on my mind for a few weeks now. I've not known which one of my personas to present to you.

As a mother, I vividly remember picking my children up on their last day of school, fighting back the tears at the school gate, knowing deep down what was about to come.

That same evening, we went to the local pub for what I said would be our 'last supper' with close friends. Little did I know that whilst we were enjoying said supper, Boris Johnson would address the nation and announce that all pubs were to close that evening. The atmosphere became intense and heavy, the sense of the unknown. It was an eerie feeling.

My eleven-year-old started to cry as we watched; he knew he wouldn't get the chance to finish primary school. The transition into comp without any preparation was daunting. No visits to his new school, no residential school trip with his friends, no leavers assembly, concert or prom night. Seven years of primary school stopped abruptly with no official goodbyes. He was heartbroken; we all were.

As a granddaughter, I didn't want to leave my nan on her own. I don't make the effort to see my family as often as I should. And being told I couldn't see them at all was gut wrenching. There were lots of tears. I sent my nan sweet treats through the post and dropped her shopping in weekly, usually timed so I could have a cuppa on the doorstep at the same time everyone came out to clap for the NHS.

I regret not spending more time with my family over the years.

My mother-in-law passed away in August and we had only seen her once in the last six months. We didn't get a chance to say our goodbyes and that will always haunt me. We were faced with exceptional circumstances out of our control, but it doesn't make the situation any easier.

Not just a granddaughter. I'm a daughter, sister, aunty, niece, cousin and a friend. A fiancé counting down the days to her wedding.

One of my happier memories was making up nearly 30 gift bags and delivering them to close family and friends so we could all celebrate my birthday virtually.

Zoom quizzes, Facetimes and so many phone calls kept us all connected over the months.

As a business owner, I had to pack up my office and face working from home for the foreseeable. Eight years of hard work... I felt like I had taken one step forward and two steps back. Not having the physical space to work from home, my kitchen soon became a makeshift office – home to the laptop and printer, client records, files, an abundance of essential stationery.

Would I survive this? How can I possibly run a business from the kitchen table with two kids at home who also need homeschooling? How can I manage my staff and our workload when we're all working remotely?

People ask how I managed to juggle everything during lockdown. But the truth is, I didn't. Work prevailed. Some incredible work achievements come to light. But behind the scenes, we survived on takeaways, lived in PJs (often unwashed), a clean and tidy house was a thing of the past and the children binged 24/7 on YouTube and Xbox. They did barely any homework.

Was I selfish to put my business before all other needs? Maybe, I can't quite decide.

As an accountant, I might not have been out on the front-line saving lives but I was working tirelessly behind the scenes saving other businesses that were providing an income for hundreds of individuals. We guided clients on government grants, assisted applications for bounce back loans, eligibility checked and sent information packs to clients who could claim via the self-employed income support scheme, navigated the job retention scheme, and sent out inspirational pick-me-ups for our clients. As a team, we went above and beyond.

Mum, granddaughter, friend, business owner and accountant – each a small part of my persona. But what about me? What is my lockdown legacy?

Empowerment. Eternal love. Kind and caring nature. Thoughtfulness. Independence. Resilience. Passion and determination. Heartbreak and sadness.

Lockdown gave me time to recharge and reflect. It reminded me of the importance of love, health and wealth, family and friends. It gave me hope during the most uncertain times. It gave me inspiration.

Iona Callaghan

Ivy Wood

LEAP YEAR PROPOSAL 2020

After six years of dating, I felt confident 2020 was going to be the year for us to move forwards.

I'd thought carefully about proposing. Not because I wanted to get married but spending the rest of our lives living closer, possibly next door to each other, appealed. We'd discussed this and were in agreement that it could work. Whilst marriage wouldn't suit because we're very different (for instance, I'm calm and tidy in the kitchen and he's like a whirlwind), we do have at least three things in common. Firstly, his mother doesn't approve of me because I'm brown, and mine wouldn't approve of him if she knew. Secondly, we're both moral, and thirdly, I love him and believe it when he says the same.

I weighed up the pros and cons, checked the leap year proposing protocol and decided to go ahead; I wanted to be sure this was the man for me. The end of February seemed appropriate. I purchased a ring, and even some fun sweets that could be slipped onto his finger as an alternative.

On the day, my heart was in my mouth as I telephoned him. He was in a good mood. I proposed.

'I love you,' he said, 'but I don't want to get married.'

He was blunt. They say the truth hurts. It did.

197

Reminding him about our discussions and explaining that my proposal was actually a kind of 'together forever without legal paperwork' made no difference. It was only afterwards when I dissected our conversation that I cringed. Why did I lighten our conversation with, 'Do you realise if you reject a woman's proposal, you have to buy her a silk gift?' Where was my pride? Who hasn't wished for hindsight as a tool in their armoury?

He came to me as usual a few weeks later, but without bearing gifts of apology, nor admitting he'd handled the situation badly. A few kind words would have acted as balm. Over the following weeks I pushed to make him understand how he'd made me feel. Occasionally he said sorry but it's a subject he actively avoided. Then along came lockdown. I think if it suited anyone, it fitted him perfectly.

My highs and lows drove me crazy and still do. Is he as unchanging as his mother who determinedly keeps him close and me at a distance? It's easier to stay in the relationship because starting afresh with someone else is invariably difficult. Recently I dreamt he died; wishful thinking maybe? He never broaches the subject of our future together. I still fancy him and he continues to say he loves me. We still laugh together and spend cosy weekends watching television. It seems neither my leap year proposal nor the threat of the pandemic have impacted the status quo. He appears to be blind to my mounting discontent. My relationship is similar to COVID-19. Only time will reveal the outcome.

Robyn Cain

BUXTON'S FIELD OF DREAMS

As marketing officer at Buxton Festival Fringe, I was involved in key decisions on how or whether to continue with this year's open-access arts festival. With the Fringe taking place in July, spring was a critical planning time. Normally we would have been closing entries and thinking about the printed programme. This year we had around 100 listings from performers who had entered before the pandemic but whose live shows might well not be possible. Anything we printed might have ended up as a work of fiction. Could it be that for the first time in 40 years there might not be a Buxton Fringe?

It was an emotional time. Some on the Fringe committee had direct experience of what the virus could do. It felt almost tasteless to be thinking about anything other than the sufferings of the nation. More and more other events were being cancelled. Even I realised that there were bigger issues than the Fringe. I remember talking to a colleague and saying that there would be some who felt the arts were far from essential. "And they'd be wrong," she replied and it was hugely gratifying to realise that it was not just me who was still hearing that insistent voice in my head maintaining that "the show must go on".

A spontaneous COVID-snake of decorated stones in the park was an added reminder that people still needed to be creative, but we were determined not to condone unsafe practices. In the end we agreed not to cancel the Fringe but to run it in whatever way was possible and responsible. Realistically that meant scrapping the printed programme, extending the entries deadline (also making it free to enter) and encouraging online events.

Knowing how difficult it would be for performers to decide what they wanted to do or could do, we decided to contact each one individually to discuss options. Although we lost events, we gained some too after we put out feelers in the local community. With just a few weeks to go before the Fringe started on July 1st we had just over 100 entries again including some physical art trails, down-the-phone micro performances and even a socially-distanced comedy show.

I felt as if a huge act of faith had paid off.

We had not cancelled the Fringe even though we knew that most of our existing acts would have to cancel. We had built our field of dreams and they had come.

In July we experienced a lot of love from performers and audiences alike. Performers really opened up to me about the challenges they were facing. There was excitement too as we talked about being at the birth of a new kind of artform – online entertainment that was neither film nor theatre. My voluntary role for the Fringe gave me something to focus on other than the latest grim COVID stats during lockdown and it reminded me that human beings are very adaptable even in the face of global adversity.

Stephanie Billen

Buxton Fringe

"It seemed people had fallen into madness!"

NO EVENTS FRIGHTEN
THE MUSE

COVID–19 in my small, unrecognised country, Lugansk
People Republic – a special event. I felt its seriousness
in May 2020. Sure, the epidemic started much earlier,
but our people, hardened by various terrible events like
Chernobyl or the Donbass war, did not attach importance to
the warnings of doctors.

Just before the May holidays (The Day of Solidarity, Victory
Day), lockdown was announced. Transport stopped moving

through the city streets. Our city isn't small – 257 km^2 – and it was devastating for our population of about 500,000 people.

Having learned bad lessons from the Donbass war 2014, people rushed to the shops, trying to grab as many products as possible. Prices soared.

It seemed people have fallen into madness! This madness touched me too, but a bit late – most shops were half empty. I wasn't too upset. I remembered 2014, when we were without money, electricity and food. I had learned to cook many plain dishes from cheap ingredients, so I was self-confident and tried to calm down some of my colleagues – mostly those who spent the war of 2014 outside Lugansk.

I decided to spend lockdown outside the city, in my dacha, a small piece of land with a small bungalow, many trees and much work that helped to take my mind off the dark thoughts.

My contact with people almost stopped. Few people live there and few could get there because of the transport collapse. I don't know why people stopped using gadgets so much at that time. In my view, it is much easier to flock together to overcome difficulty.

After some days, I ran out of bread. It is 5 km to the nearest shop. We used our car, but were afraid to use the usual route as penalties were promised for breaking the rules. My husband and I drove through the cemetery and through the forest. The sudden appearance of a hare made me laugh. The animal was shocked with our mad driving over bumps and holes! Nobody had driven there before, I think.

In a merry mood, we came to 'civilisation' and saw that civilisation was alive. People were walking, but at least still moving, without any fear of being penalised. Of course, masks became an accessory, antiseptics replaced perfume, and lipstick became a completely unnecessary attribute.

At that time the first fatal outcomes of the disease began.

My 52-year-old friend died. I was shocked. During the funeral, I saw rows of prepared graves in the cemetery – prepared for the consequences of COVID–19. Thanks to God, most of them not needed. In terms of statistics, today 2,995 have been infected in the country and 262 patients have died.

May was the most tense month for us. We live with some limits in freedom due to the confrontation with Ukraine. We have the curfew, yet we are moving with caution due to possible mines, so a pandemic hasn't thrilled us too much.

I know some people who were overloaded with fears, but not many. I think nervous people left our place with the Donbass war beginning and those who stayed learned to control their feelings.

I can say that I've learnt some useful things: I mastered computer programs to work with my students online. I have trained my immune system with herbal teas and gymnastics. I wrote many poems – no events frighten the muse!

Larisa Bekresheva

*"I learnt to adapt and make
the most of everything."*

LOCKDOWN 2020 AND BEYOND!

My favourite things in life are being with my family, meeting up with my friends, going to the theatre, walking in the great outdoors, and travelling to London. Just a simple life I lead and these things keep me sane and make me happy.

Life in lockdown took everything I needed to function away from me – or did it?

I learnt to adapt and make the most of everything I could continue to do.

I have been given, I feel, a time to sit back and reflect, rest and relax and stop the need to fill my diary – I was constantly planning. I am appreciating my home more, discovering local walks, making more time for selfcare, reading, writing, watching films and actually cooking – I've become a Gousto cook!

I've watched our girls become more independent, both very different. One adapting to work fulltime from home and still managing to complete a college course in HR, passing with a distinction and enjoying London life at a slower pace. The other juggling homeschooling and continuing to work as a carer, out there in all weathers looking after our elderly folk.

Our grandchildren have been so resilient, from clapping on the doorstep in support of the NHS, to doorstep visits to Grandma and knowing why not to hug, to socially distance and wash their hands. They have made us proud. My hubbie has continued to work throughout, not missing a day! And when our 30th wedding anniversary plans of a London weekend with a champagne theatre trip at the Palladium were cancelled we still enjoyed the day, the two of us eating sausage rolls and having a cuppa in the car in the rain in Snowdonia!

Cara got home from London to spend Christmas with us; it was a very special one after not being able to do our regular trips to see her.

I've connected with my brothers and sisters and their families over Zoom, celebrated birthdays virtually and arranged bingo and scavenger hunts for the little and big kids too!

I've stayed connected with old friends, having regular virtual cuppas, walk and talks, Zoom evenings with wine, and I've actually made more new friends this last year than ever before, both in and out of work.

I'm grateful I've been able to volunteer and support the COVID-19 vaccination programme, which was very rewarding and good for my mental health to get out there and do something useful.

So whilst there has been a lot of sadness in the world, and with some of my friends going through extremely sad and heartbreaking situations, I'm glad I've been able to stay strong enough to be able to support them and gain some positivity from this strange situation we have all found ourselves in. I'm cautiously optimistic that we will take all the positives and learn from the nightmare of 2020 and all enjoy a safe and happy future, learning to live in the new normal. In the words of Dr Kathryn Mannix, 'Shining your own light gives hope and direction to other people. In this dark time we can all keep a light on. You never know when your light is someone else's reason to keep hoping.'

My light is staying on and shining brightly. :)

So lucky to have had a summer 2020 holiday to make up for the many months of no hugs!

Sandra Smith

"Above all, lockdown has shown the importance of human connection."

CRUCIAL CONVERSATIONS
THAT CONNECT AND COUNT

Whilst a unique experience for us all, lockdown has been an enlightening one for me, full of new opportunities and self-actualisation.

Unable to pursue my normal creative outlet of directing theatrical productions, I wanted to do something that would keep lines of communication open and conversations going; something that would make a difference to the lives of many and which tied in with what theatre is all about – telling stories, educating, sharing ideas and values, evoking passions and emotions, and taking people on a journey.

Hence my 'In Conversation With' talks with people from all walks of life, giving them the platform to share their stories, personality and vision, and use social media for good to inspire and build community and to share important issues like mental health.

We have been able to stream these to Facebook and also share them on my YouTube channel, but an exciting development was getting my own page in the prestigious *Cheshire Life*, allowing me to share the occasional story in print.

What have these conversations taught me? I have learnt so much, but not just about the people themselves.

Firstly, there is the power of different types of storytelling. We are all wired for storytelling since our early years of being read to. But there is also such a power in verbal and visual storytelling which is what these conversations have given – to teach, inspire and share experiences that resonate with others. It has given the opportunity to learn from each other and give a sense of shared experiences.

It has also taught me that keeping conversations and communication going is so important for our own mental well-being and that of others; and that sharing those stories of our own adversity can provide support and hope to others.

Above all, lockdown has shown the importance of human connection, and the devastating impact of having our physical connections removed, leading to isolation and loneliness and affecting our mental health.

Kalini Kent

Confident Communication Consultancy and Coaching

212

GIFT OR TRAGEDY?

W e have all said nobody could make an actual world lockdown up! At first it was surreal, eerie, confusing and exciting. I personally thought it was a permission to take a break, seeing it as an opportunity to spend time with my husband and focus on improving systems and practices in my business.

This is my second career and I am a trained Foot Health Practitioner (In my previous life I was a psychotherapist for almost 30 years). I've been running my foot clinic for two years and I was starting to work out who my ideal patients were and what niche treatments I wanted to develop.

We spent time on home projects, then looking forward to our hourly walk, which sometimes took longer and we felt like lawbreaking teenagers. My husband, Paul, created a lovely small garden out the back for me to grow some vegetables, some of which survived and some didn't. I generally felt incredibly content. However, my husband struggled with his depression as he was not used to settling down. I always said he was 1000 miles an hour.

On the 12th June, I received a call from my youngest son (26 years old) to say he had been diagnosed with testicular cancer. He had not long completed his Doctorate, got a really good job in Surrey, and was becoming a great  success within the firm. It was incredibly scary during this time because COVID was still rife, especially in the hospitals, plus the media hype was that they were limiting treatments for cancer treatments. Thankfully he had an amazing consultant and was told to self-isolate. Within 10 days of diagnosis, he had his left testicle removed, then a month later had a large hit of chemotherapy and has since recovered. However, he has to have blood tests and checks every 2 months. He's back a work, bought a new car and has had a raise.

During this time my husband's depression increased and on Friday, 13th November he told me he wanted to be on his own so he moved out to his sister's and is currently looking for a place to live. It was a complete shock to me and his whole family who adore me. At the same time, my middle son was diagnosed COVID positive and has had symptoms but so far hasn't got any worse.

Whilst it's a complete devastation losing my husband, I am surprised at how I'm not completely falling apart. Work has been very busy and I have been able to have a laugh with my amazing patients. I continue to see myself as very lucky and blessed. I am surrounded by amazing friends and family and my Christian faith has been paramount to me in keeping me steady and strong. I choose to continue seeing joy in every day because I have so much to be thankful for.

Sue Quinton

Sue Quinton Foot Clinic

"I was troubled by the large number of my colleagues who had been furloughed, a word I'd never heard pre-virus."

LOCKDOWN – LOVING OR LOATHING

H ey, how hard can it be to be stuck in the house you have chosen as your home, with the people you 'love'?

Well, I now know, that's easy to ask and hard to answer.

You see, life is complicated: work, locations, relationships, the odd crisis and things that I've not thought too much about until now.

Day one, I'm still working, that's 'normal', but the devilish threat of the virus is already showing its face. 'Normal' is about to melt away. People are the lifeblood of a fundraiser working for a charity: kind people, generous people, people who care and want to make a difference. That lifeblood was about to be drained by the evil virus. Key sources of funding were in clear and present danger, no events, no face-to-face meetings, no shops, a loss of 80% of our revenue. This virus was going to deliver us a catastrophic blow! I was turning every stone to generate every £ available. Is this the new normal? What does the future look like?

I was troubled by the large number of my colleagues who had been furloughed, a word I'd never heard pre-virus. What initially appeared to be utopia by those who were still working quickly became a nightmare for those who were furloughed. Their professional life was very much on hold; working is much more than just getting paid. As 'outsiders', their perception or reality, official contact with them waned very rapidly, as did their sense of self-worth. The impact of furlough on mental health and general wellbeing has yet to be professionally reviewed. "Why didn't I make the team?" "Why am I less valuable?" There will be many more questions to ask and much to learn in the days and months ahead.

On the upside, I'm so privileged to live in a beautiful part of the world, space to wander safely alone, no crowds, fields and wildlife outside the front door. A house with enough space for the family to find their own space on inclement days. We aren't free of the virus' grasp but we're safer than many others. But thoughts of a 'gilded cage' are ever present, prisoners in paradise with many family members, friends and colleagues out of touch. Technology to the rescue? Zoom/Teams video calls (other tech is available), but they don't do hugs or other social contact that we've always taken for granted.

Dealing with life's challenges becomes more challenging, emotionally draining, and at times scary!

My 20-year-old 'Baby Girl', halfway through her nursing degree, was called up to the front-line working the wards. "OMG, she's too young, too vulnerable!" I/we feel vulnerable because it is morally and ethically a no-brainer, but we don't want her in harm's way. She tests positive for the virus within a week of working, with three patients testing positive on her Green (non COVID-19) ward, so no PPE. A mixture of terror and anger gripped me. Fortunately, her symptoms continued to be mild and we all tested negative, but we'd brushed with the virus, so not feeling so safe now!

Lockdown reflections: fresher air, peace and tranquillity – thanks to a dramatic reduction in travel. Lessons to be learnt about our personal and professional worlds? You bet! Major challenges to overcome as we establish the new normal: How do we put human contact back into our lives? How do we survive personally and professionally, given the ongoing threats to our health and the economy? Obsessing on the 'small stuff', such as "What's for tea? Who used all the hot water, I need a shower?" is clearly thrown into sharp relief.

Beverley Bradley

Ty Gobaith Children's Hospice

"My philosophy for lockdown life has been sanity over vanity."

WHEN LOCKDOWN BECOMES YOUR LIFT UP!

f you'd suggested to me this time last year that I should work from my garage, in a 10x7 space with no windows, extremes of temperature from really cold to boiling hot and be enjoying all of that, I'd have thought you'd have gone mad!

Life in lockdown has been liberating. Faced with dwindling class numbers for my fitness business in the run up to the pandemic lockdown (many clients already self-isolating to protect themselves and their loved ones), I had to step outside my comfort zone to consider a future without face-to-face personal contact and embrace technology!

My Time for Change (the wellbeing, nutrition and health arm to my business) has always been an online service. However, with the world facing a new wake-up call to health, wellbeing and immunity, the programme has thrived and given a platform to shout more about how much it can help improve your mental and physical health. What we eat affects our coping mechanisms, stress levels, immunity and metabolic health markers.

I pivoted my fitness business quickly, taking my classes online the week before lockdown, from thereon the Zoom Room was created.

Thanks to my business partner, Mindy Cowap, I was encouraged to enter a cyber room, and that has been a life saver not only for my business but for the health and wellbeing of my clients. They have had uninterrupted easy access to my fitness classes.

My philosophy for lockdown life has been sanity over vanity and I gave clients structure to their lives, but also a taste of normality, seeing familiar faces and exercising amongst their friends. Having a virtual place to go, a date in the diary, routine and most importantly, still looking after their wellbeing.

Within 24 hours I had turned a class in a village hall to a class from my garage where I could still see, chat and monitor technique and make adjustments on an individual basis.

Lockdown has highlighted just how important our mental and emotional wellbeing is.

No longer is not having time to exercise a reason not to exercise, never has it been easier to access a fitness class on your terms. My classes are available to everyone, at anytime, anywhere. You are moments from your shower and your next meal. Working out in whatever workout gear takes your fancy (even your birthday suit!).

Due to the incredible feedback and success and because so many are reluctant to go back to old ways, classes will remain online. For so many it's flexible and suits their life far better.

The future is exciting as lockdown has accelerated the opportunities and experiences that I can offer clients!

Emma Wilson

Emma Wilson Fitness

"I sure will look back with more smiles than tears."

LIFE AS A HOTELIER DURING 2020/21

So, I'm sitting at home having a cup of tea in front of the TV and on comes the news that tourists are having to isolate in an hotel in Tenerife. It's February 2020. I turn to my husband and discuss what would happen if that was to take place at our hotel. Who would be liable for costs, the guest or us? Went to bed unnerved but put it to the back of our minds.

Things were changing, there seemed to be real concern over this virus, scary news reporting. Time to have a sit down with the staff to see how everyone was feeling and start to implement extra cleaning protocols, hand sanitiser at the ready. Then the inevitable happened, the phone calls were coming in to cancel and request for refunds. This was particularly difficult for some members of the team so I took to the phones to handle the requests. I will admit there were a number of times I only just about manged to hold back the tears. Then the announcement from the Prime Minister to say the country was going into lockdown; my heart sank but I reminded myself I must think about the staff and try to put on a brave face.

Then the challenge began.

The next few weeks were filled with securing extra funding via new government schemes launched and Banc Wales, hoping we could secure enough to keep us afloat, not knowing for how long we were going to be closed.

First challenge completed, we then made the decision to redecorate some bedrooms and public areas so they would be fresh and revitalised for when we could welcome guests back.

Having worked in corporate hotels in our past lives, we made the decision that a brand was more important now than ever and joined Best Western. This required us to update and change our Property Management System (PMS), so something else to keep me busy. There were some specific requirements needed to join, all done over video chat, something we soon realised was going to be the way forward for communicating to the outside world.

Mid-July came and finally here in North Wales we could open to guests again, which brought some apprehension but we knew that we had put the necessary procedures in place to keep ourselves, guests and staff safe. Bookings were better than expected, and with the addition of the Government's Eat Out to Help Scheme our restaurant also received a much-needed boost. It was great to welcome back old faces and welcome new ones too, and with the procedures put in place, they commented on how safe they felt. We had some staffing issues, but worked our way through with a smile on our face for 10 weeks.

The first of October came and bang, lockdown again. With travel restrictions and fire-breaks, England and Wales working to different agendas, we had no option but to close again.

With the help of a Welsh Government grant, we continue to invest, we have updated a third of our bathrooms and are renewing equipment in our kitchen. When we reopen, we will offer a range of our own in-house aged steaks and our restaurant will now be known as Samphire Chophouse & Seafood Brasserie @ The Cae Mor Hotel.

In summary, 2020 was a challenging year for everyone, but the support of friends at *Network She* has helped me through some challenging moments on more than one occasion. Although still closed at the time of writing, we look forward to a more positive 2021 and I sure will look back with more smiles than tears.

Sheryl Viercant

Cae Mor Hotel

"I stayed up watching the news into the night."

ONCE IN A LIFETIME

The unknown of March held me back from pressing the 'proceed to payment' button on my Qantas shopping bag – Brisbane to Manchester return – for a once in a lifetime trip. A trip in the making for 100 years! That of Nana's 100th birthday.

I had held back due to an uncertain situation at work and an expected redundancy before Christmas 2019. However, as work dragged on I had March in the back of my mind, that it would all pan out with pristine timing, to take the redundancy money, go for my extended trip back to the UK and enjoy some quality time with my nana. It didn't matter at all that it would be a last minute booking, I just knew I would be there.

As the unknown at work marched on I was left with a last minute request to take three weeks off to go overseas. Once authorised, I booked in ready to 'proceed', conveniently getting the same flight there as my mum, who had booked her ticket well in advance. Leaving the screen open on my laptop, I put the kids to bed and talked to them about me going away. They were excited for me going (I'm sure in a nice way!) – they think it's amazing that their great nana is 100!

Then, what seemed out of the blue, an announcement on the news that there was a pandemic blooming, the dreaded COVID. It was crazy to think then that it would take over the world, and of course most people's reaction was that it would 'blow over'. I stayed up watching the news into the night and then started Googling away. My heart sank, selfishly at the time for my own pursuit.

The next day it seemed the whole world had changed overnight. The news was now saying that Australian borders were closing and any travelers would not be able to return to the country. What the hell was going on? Australia's reaction seemed hasty, especially compared to the UK. There were mutterings amongst the community that it had been blown out of proportion and everyone seemed to have a story of how their relatives were going to be trapped abroad.

Here is the most important lady in our lives, rocking 100 and sitting with the Queen, who managed to make it to North Wales amidst a pandemic.

The horror stories rolled in and the proceed to payment never happened. Mum cancelled her flight. I felt so angry at the time, so upset, it seemed so unfair. All I thought about was my nana and how for a lifetime we had imagined if she got to 100 what a party we would have. I am absolutely sure she had thought this too.

Looking back now, I think of all those lives lost, all those families devastated. Then the impact not only on the immediate future but on the next generations. It makes you realise just how grateful we are to still have Nana in our lives and cherish our families and friends.

In hindsight, my initial anger at the Australian Government, and in particular Queensland, is replaced with respect for the quick decisions they made and ultimately saving thousands of lives.

As it stands today, 21st October 2020, Queensland can report six lives lost, around 1160 cases, 0 reported cases at present. In Australia there have been 907 deaths in total and minimal new cases. What is most important is that all states have a handle on the 'track and trace' and tests are proactive and plentiful.

What is a struggle from a personal point of view is being on the other side of the world when our friends and family are amidst the unknown and there are no plans to reunite in the immediate future. It feels overwhelming not to have that choice anymore, especially when you feel cheated that you weren't at such a significant milestone with the family.

Lisa Haydn Davis

WE CLAPPED FOR CARERS

HARNESSING THE CLAP

When my newly self-employed world caved in overnight, I scratched around applying for supermarket jobs that didn't exist along with thousands of other folks in the same boat. Five weeks into lockdown, I struck lucky. After four days of training and shadowing, I was issued a uniform, some basic PPE and I was deemed competent enough to be let loose as a carer for individuals with dementia.

I am completely in awe of those people, mostly women, who take up a career as a carer. They are paid less, treated badly by employers and treated as second class citizens. We clapped for carers for weeks, but nothing has changed for them. I was lucky, I subsequently got an admin role and am now sat in my home in front of a computer, safe and well.

Not all carers care as much as the ones I worked with, and when you look at the way they are treated, it's not really that surprising. Agencies have a massive turnover of staff and are not that fussy about who does the job.

As a carer, you often work from 7am until 10pm but only get paid for nine hours. You walk into a client's house, clock on via a microchip and your allocated time starts. If a house call is supposed to last 30 minutes but lasts 45 because that person cannot get washed and dressed in that timeframe, then you work the extra 15 minutes unpaid.

Most agencies allow five minutes to get between calls, unpaid. These five minutes involve clocking out of the house, walking to your car, getting in your car, driving to the next house, getting out of your car (with the relevant PPE), getting into the next house (which would involve getting a key out of a lock box) and then clocking in. As you can guess, you are always running behind schedule as five minutes is not enough.

The agencies kindly pay you 30p per mile to cover travel between calls. This is a loophole in legislation which means they don't need to pay an hourly rate. They give you several breaks too. Unpaid of course and always conveniently placed so that your 20-minute break ends up being five as you over-ran on all the previous calls and travelling time. Lunchtimes are the most successful for the agencies. The most difficult clients would be placed just before lunch or at night-time, so that if you over-ran by 30 minutes (as is often the case), you were not affecting any other clients, just your own unpaid time. There were often 45-minute and 60-minute gaps between calls, all unpaid gaps of course, so a liking for sitting around in your car is a must.

My lockdown experience has given me a lifetime of respect and admiration for carers. I have mentioned the word 'unpaid' five times! Surely that is not right? Let's harness that clapping and make sure social care workers are not forgotten.

Carolyn Eve

BEING CREATIVE AND STAYING CREATIVE

A s a freelance illustrator, I work from home so in a number of ways my working life was largely unchanged when we were asked to stay home. I also teach art, as an after-school art club tutor, at two local primary schools. I really enjoy teaching but when the schools closed my teaching was put on hold and as yet I have no date as to when I may be teaching again.

For my own well-being, I started to post art projects for children on my social media. I hoped that the projects would help parents who found themselves at home with children to educate and to entertain.

In doing this, I was not alone as during this time there was an extraordinary outburst of creativity from around the world. Artists and makers offered creative ideas and challenges to people who were at home with more time and many with children at home as well. The popularity of these ideas and challenges clearly showed that people were seeking the positive feelings that can result from play and creativity. Creativity involves problem solving and these creative ideas and challenges offered people an opportunity to solve problems at a time when the larger problems we were all facing could not be and continue not to be solved.

The comments that I received about my projects led me to work on a book aimed at parents and at educators. The book is being written in response to our extraordinary times and in response to my interest in visual thinking.

Loo roll tube fox

As I have been writing the chapters the situation regarding the pandemic and the resulting effects on our society have been changing. In the staying home period, the collective experience provided us all with support. However, since we came out of our houses into a much more uncertain place, the so-called surge capacity of us all has been severely tested.

My son has experienced the chaos of A-Levels and subsequently the new reality of university life, with only two sessions of online teaching per week. My daughter has experienced finishing her degree online, a virtual graduation and a very uncertain employment market.

It has been extremely challenging for our young people but I have also witnessed a profound change in my elderly mother. She has always been a very positive person but she has struggled hugely with understanding the pandemic and living with it. Each generation has faced the same issues and others of their own.

In my work, I am at my happiest when working on a brief. As the year has gone by my commissioned work has stalled and in a way I have set my own briefs with the projects and with writing the book. As we have all had to adapt to the loss of our old world, I think that we have all had to learn to set our own briefs, with the hope that we will be able to fulfil them in this new world.

Lucy Monkman

"I'm dedicating my Lockdown Legacy to the 5.82 million small businesses across the UK, most of whom are just trying to survive and maintain their place in their local communities."

TO THE SMALL BUSINESSES

We know the world will be a very different place at such a point when we are able to start to rebuild post-pandemic. As a behaviourist and consumer expert, I take past data and trends and try to overlay with what we understand will be the opportunities and changes of the future.

We're already feeling the huge economic impact, as well as the social hurt and pain of the lives lost and the huge strain on our health system and key workers.

We're seeing industries like entertainment, hospitality and retail suffer beyond measure, with many businesses of all shapes and sizes simply unable to keep going.

Some of the greatest acts of business generosity have been from the smallest of businesses, and I am hopeful that one of the trends we will witness as a result is more support for the small businesses that have rallied to make a difference.

The Javeds in Falkirk made international news as the story of their kindness was told. The couple own a corner shop and invested £4,000 in 2,000 packs of necessities for the older people in their community.

There are many stories of cafés that donated meals to key workers, fashion businesses that produced PPE and distilleries that ditched the gin in favour of hand-sanitiser.

Many of these businesses didn't think twice in leaping to make a difference.

I wasn't surprised at this out-pouring of support from the independent business community and have been an admirer of the sheer hard work, determination and passion demonstrated by small-business owners since I started in the world of work.

When I think of the skills I use in serving my own clients, it is less of the academia from the renowned business schools and more the influence of my nan that helps me make the difference every day – a shopkeeper with brilliant service values, playing the role of both service advisor and counsellor.

And that is a tale from the past that I hope will go on to influence our future. That the smallest of business operators can teach the biggest of businesses a thing or two about what the heart of a business should look like.

When I founded my business consultancy, Insight with Passion, I was determined to support small businesses and founded the Access for All scheme, which sees us donate 20% of time back to supporting small businesses and community organisations, free of charge. Over the past decade we've helped over 1,500 small businesses, working with organisations like Welcome to Yorkshire and the Farm Retail Association. In 2020 we upped the giveback to 40%, spending hours on the phone supporting business owners and hosting free online seminars and workshops to not only share our expertise but also to provide a morale boost for small businesses and to show them that they matter.

I'm the proud founder of Indie Business Live, the UK's leading small business festival, and was delighted with the outpouring of support from small businesses, the public and famous faces alike.

Kate Hardcastle, MBE

Insight with Passion

"Priority – buy wine!"

MISSION ACCOMPLISHED

Sunday, March 1st 2020, I drove my husband, David, to the airport where he was headed back to the UK. Little did we know that the next time we would see each other would be July 2nd.

On Saturday, 14th March, my life turned upside down.

David had been on a flight from London to Fuerteventura to start our relocation journey back to the UK. Instead, the flight was turned around mid-flight and Coronavirus had well and truly made its mark in Central Europe.

Spain went into lockdown, one of the toughest in the world. We had army roadblocks, police checking where you had been and for how long, no exercise allowed at all, unable to walk the dogs more than 50 metres and no one, other than Spanish residents or citizens, were allowed in.

For months, like many others, I sat on my sofa and didn't move.

Fast forward to June. There was a glimmer of hope. Spain was starting to open up. If you had the right papers, you could travel to the mainland. Then the green light, ferries were to restart from Spain to the UK at the end of June. We still had one problem – David couldn't get to me.

One morning I woke up and put on my *Network She* big girl pants and decided that I was going to make the journey from the Canaries to the UK on my own. Me, my van and two dogs. What could go wrong?!

June 24th, I started the epic journey home.

Fuerteventura – Gran Canaria – Huelva – 38 hours at sea, with two dogs. What an experience! It didn't get off to the best start as I had booked an Airbnb on the fifth floor with a tiny lift. The doggies decided they didn't like lifts!

The next morning, I couldn't find the port so paid a taxi driver to get me there.

I reached the mainland on Friday, 26th June.

Priority – buy wine! Mission accomplished.

I then started the monumental drive up through Spain. 900km of Tarmac stretched out in front of me, Portugal to my left, Spain to my right, two days to do it in. After 10 hours of driving, I reached my first night hotel and what a dream it was. I was met with bread and wine. What more do you need in life?

Day 2 took me through the mountains. Northern Spain is breathtaking and I will go back under less stressful conditions. By Sunday night I had reached Santander. The end was in sight; several tears were shed and a large red was consumed.

My ferry to the UK was due to sail on Monday 29th at 15.00. Guess what... it got cancelled! After calls to the Foreign Office and the British Embassy, I was given a place on a repatriation ferry on Wednesday, 1st July.

On 2nd July, I reached the UK and I was finally reunited with Dave.

Priority – Fish and chips... MISSION ACCOMPLISHED!

Claire Evans

"COVID-19, the invisible enemy."

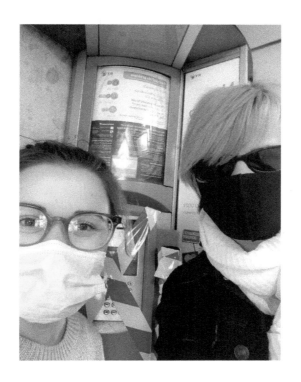

THE FIRST JOURNEY

How bizarre coming from a woman that has travelled up and down the UK on multiple occasions, every month for years, to be so anxious about leaving her home. Four months of semi-isolation, cocooned in the safety of four walls, changes your perspective of life. I am the first to admit, it became a blissful reprieve from the hectic business lifestyle I was leading.

Why? I ask myself, heart hammering, hands shaking.

The occasion? On July 6th 2020 you were able to travel for more than five miles in North Wales after four months of 'stay local'. My daughter travelled up from London to finally come home after six months on the frontline as an Operating Department Practitioner (ODP) in a London hospital. The emotions throughout this time have been extreme in the least. My first journey to see my son... in beautiful Brighton.

I'm not one to miss my eldest children; I am proud they have grown up to be independent, productive members of society... that is, in the knowledge that I can jump on a train, drive to go and see them. The freedom that we had stopped overnight to be replaced with an ache so deep. Trapped, me in one country, two of my children in another. The irony of living in the United Kingdom with a pandemic that respects no borders and politicians point scoring.

COVID–19, the invisible enemy, moving stealthily from person to person, no respect for class, religion or culture. Adjacent train seats cordoned off, empty carriages, food trollies supplying overpriced dry sandwiches, coffees and refreshments a thing of the past.

I found myself on Crewe platform, just staring, taking in the masked people, some brave souls barefaced, one metre or more apart (if you can, thanks Boris for your clarity). Gone the jostling crowds, pushing to board the train and grab any available seat/piece of floor/leaning space. Hello England, we meet again, like viewing you from the eyes of a young child.

Boarding the London train, I note not a Virgin train any more, new franchises, the introductory 'Hi, I'm a toilet' recording removed.

A much more civilised and dignified journey, though solitary behind the mask.

'How do you describe a mugger these days if everyone is wearing a face covering?'

Random thoughts just pop into your mind in these strange times. Looking out of the window as the train speeds to its destination, the landscape looks so normal, yet we are a society changed beyond recognition. Announcements advising on social distancing replace the cheery conductor, machines replacing humans – they are immune to the virus, we are not yet.

My darling son, I'm on my way and yes, I will be giving you a very long hug, after washing my hands for two verses of Happy Birthday.

Your next stop is Euston. Thank you for travelling with Arriva Wales. Please be advised that social distancing rules must be adhered to.

Julie Williams

The Coaching Den

"Times are unprecedented."

WORKSPACE, DESK SPACE, DINING TABLE

irst days of lockdown I am overwhelmed with a sense of deep heart-wrenching love for my family, joy at having some of them return home, and guilt that I am enjoying this time whilst others lose their jobs, suffer hardship and loss, get sick or, in some cases, die.

Times are unprecedented. Futures unknown. Daily news bulletins here in New Zealand talk of more cases and more deaths worldwide... but I feel safe, and calm and lucky.

I sit at the dining table, my new desk, which is covered in books and papers, laptop, devices. I sit at my workstation and stare out the window. I watch a spider spin a web and I bask in the last days of summer.

Sitting at my new workspace, I welcome colleagues into my home via Zoom. Initially I am conscious of the old shabby curtains that sit as my backdrop and so I experiment with a sofa location, a plain backdrop, a favourite painting, and revert quite quickly to the original and most convenient workspace despite the shabby curtains. It reminds me of when we first came to visit the house and I recall thinking, if we do buy it, this room will have to be redecorated... and I guess it will, eventually.

Routines develop as we learn to live together again, sharing space and time, fun and laughter, stories, games and meals.

Meal time means clearing my workspace. Workspace, desk space, dining table. But time is fluid, pressure is less, deadlines become flexible as we focus on hauora, health and wellbeing. Hauora for whanau, hauora for ako hoa mahi, hauora for te tangata; physical, spiritual, emotional and social wellbeing for all people.

The birds seem to sing more loudly at this time of Rāhui. The spiders seem to spin more beautifully. The dogs benefit from two or three walks instead of their usual rushed one and as such are beginning to think they have more rights and privileges than they actually do, spending time inside with us. As autumn rolls in, the temperature drops and the days start to become shorter.

Time passes, routines become established.

The table, desk, workspace holds onto all aspects of its many functions. A pencil sitting beside a knife, the pepper grinder amidst my books, paint and crumbs, plates and diary.

The garden gives us food, the chickens lay us eggs, the flour runs out... and I queue for more. We light the autumnal fire and nestle in. We have family gatherings in a virtual space, and momentarily find ourselves more involved in each other's lives, despite closed borders, as we channel into each other's living space.

Last night's empty glass,
glinting in the morning sun,
a cereal bowl on top of
yesterday's notes, the dining
table, the desk, the workspace,
where last night finished and
today begins and summer
gives way to autumn.

Ruth Foulkes

BUT STILL WE CELEBRATED

Happy Birthday to: Jack Mears, Hannah Mackie, Ella Hastings, Freya Burleigh, Ethan Hastings and Alex Mackie.

BIRTHDAY BINGO

W e weren't quite sure how this Lockdown Birthday Bingo for 30 plus friends was going to work. Technology has a way of not playing ball when you want it to, plus the fact a lot of our friends had NEVER played bingo – I know, hard to believe. But, it all went well.

It was good fun and some people came away with a lot of money. Definitely a great way to see friends, but doesn't beat the real thing... obvs.

Teresa Bushell

"We are on a mission to discover the world together now!"

LOVE IN UNEXPECTED PLACES

think my story is not far from a miraculous one. I'll tell it from the beginning.

During lockdown, everyone knew the rules and the importance of obeying them. Understanding the gravity of the situation, everybody went into a form of survival mode and tested out their resilience resources. We set off into lockdown with rigid plans and a feeling of emptiness.

Luckily we could exercise. Being able to walk and run outside felt like a ticket to expand the horizons, and I'd spend a lot of time wandering along the coast of the Irish sea, where the waves whispered with their eternal wisdom.

After a while I added a detour to a neighbour's house – my friend lived there with her little daughter. I used to stop for a quick greeting through the window and did a few star jumps outside, trying to make the most of my exercise time.

With lockdown you appreciate any freedom you can get and sometimes behave like a crazy teenager.

The child behind the window noticed the strange activity from a certain energetic person and was quite curious about the world outside the home.

Once the little girl remembered my star jumps and she started joining in enthusiastically. And that's how we were introduced – Marina, the star jump performer and Lizaveta, the little girl. Though the jumping person outside was a bit similar to all those characters on any other screen in the modern world which Lizaveta was accustomed too.

The real discovery happened when her mum went for a walk and popped to Marina's garden. Surprise! Marina was a person, not just something on a screen – that was a discovery in itself for Lizaveta. We could literally run in the garden and throw stones in that pond (the size of the bath for you and me – the size of a lake for Lizaveta).

After a few visits, Marina's house was established as an important destination and parents were instructed to go for a walk to 'Marina'. The world was so colourful in Marina's kingdom where Lizaveta could climb the trees, taste raspberries from the bush, throw different things into the pond to see if they could float and go to the wild parts of the garden with a torch to explore.

I have to say here that Lizaveta has wonderful loving parents, active, with plenty of entertainment, including their own garden. This little girl, being just over two years old, had chosen her own friend, independently. What a spirit!

When we moved out of the lockdown, we walked hand in hand, doing rounds of the pond, 'the woods' and climbing trees. Lizaveta would munch a piece of cake or pie, as her mum said it must be the best in world at Marina's. When the rounds were finished and everything in the garden had been checked and discussed, Lizaveta would signal her parents – off she went! And till the next time!

We are on a mission to discover the world together now!

Marina Kogan

Kogan Coaching

"Clear the corridors, we have a COVID patient!"

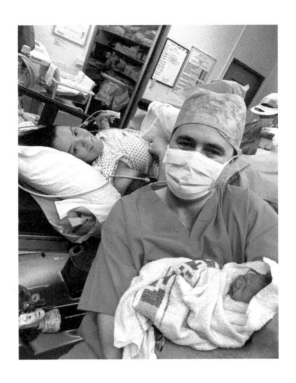

A LOCKDOWN ARRIVAL

O n the eve of March the 16th, 2020, my husband and I arrived at a holiday cottage in York for our last holiday before our baby girl was due. We had just got unpacked in our beautiful holiday lodge and settled down to watch television after our long journey from Wales. This was the moment my pregnancy journey changed and suddenly everything became very different.

From this moment on, pregnant ladies were in the vulnerable persons' category, those who were to shield from COVID-19 in their homes. So this is where it all started.

That Friday I had to attend maternity triage due to the lack of movement of my baby. My husband and I were sat in triage with a CTG machine monitoring baby's movements – a very scary time. Suddenly, a midwife appeared who told my husband that visitors were no longer allowed in the hospital and that he would have to leave the hospital grounds and he had to go with immediate effect – not knowing what was happening with our baby.

He spent several hours in the hospital car park over the days leading up to our daughter's arrival. I attended scans alone and was also admitted into hospital at 32 weeks pregnant for a 48-hour period. This was probably the closest I got to seeing Coronavirus and it was absolutely terrifying without the support of my husband. I had to go for a CT scan. On my way down from the ward I heard a male nurse shout "Clear the corridors, we have a COVID patient!" Right before my eyes a frail looking gentleman in a mask was wheeled through to be scanned before me.

For weeks after the scan I was absolutely terrified that I had caught COVID-19 and that my unborn child could be in danger, but thankfully we did not catch the virus.

After many weeks of going back and forth to the hospital when the whole of Wales was in lockdown, the day finally arrived – the day I was admitted to be induced to bring my baby into the world at 38 weeks. After two days of being in hospital alone, having to speak to my husband through the hospital window and after many complications, the day was finally here – the day I gave birth to our precious baby girl, our girl who was born in the middle of a global pandemic, and she is absolutely perfect.

The days after coming home are usually filled with midwife visits and non-stop family visits. We had no experience of this. We were in our little bubble of three and actually, we felt like the luckiest parents alive. We got to have our perfect baby girl all to ourselves for the first eight weeks of her life until lockdown restrictions were loosened.

Giving birth to my first baby during COVID-19 lockdown was the most terrifying yet perfect scenario.

Sarah Elliott

"We loved and lost."

SHE LIVES IN US ALL

My mother (Caroline Bellis) was born in North Wales, lived most of her life in Mold, then at Marleyfield care home Buckley since 2001.

She married my dad, Ted, at the start of the Second World War and lived above his family fruit and veg shop in the High street. During the war, she worked at Rhydymwyn munitions factory making mustard gas bombs while Dad was in the RAF. The part of the job she disliked was taking the bombs on trollies to the tunnels. She'd say, "I used to hate it. Bats would come in. There was hardly any light on in the middle of the night, very eerie. Not a nice job really." She worked there for five years but had to finish before the end of the war as she was having a baby, my sister.

Mum later worked as a kitchen assistant at Bryn Gwalia school, Mold, until she retired. My parents had three grandchildren and four great grandchildren.

Dad passed away 25 years ago and Mum went to the home five years later. She's been so happy there and we used to take her out shopping and for tea weekly.

Bless her, it's been a hard year, but she passed away COVID and pain-free, peacefully in her cosy bed. I hadn't been able to touch her since March and couldn't see her after Christmas because of the restrictions.

She was a very sociable person who loved music, singing, dancing and a party. She was dearly loved by all who knew her and I am blessed to have had such an icon for a mum.

She lives in us all.

Moira Owen

"OUR OLDEST WWII WORKER PASSES AWAY"

We regret to inform you that Caroline Bellis passed away peacefully on Saturday 30th January 2021, aged 104, at her care home Marleyfield House, Buckley.

Caroline was a great friend of Rhydymwyn Valley History Society (RVHS) and was a VIP guest at the re-opening of the tunnels.

Her family were so proud of her war work at Rhydymwyn and so touched by the high esteem she was held in by the Society. She was always given the warmest of welcomes during her visits and her family will continue the connection to ensure that the link is not broken.

I suppose the enduring memory we will have of her in her later years is her joie-de-vivre.

Caroline's memory will linger with us into our future.

THE GOATS OF LLANDUDNO

Dusk has fallen
On abandoned streets,
Not a sound to be heard
No person to meet.

Then came the clatter
Of hooves on the floor,
An avalanche of white
Furry miscreants explore.

The Goats of Llandudno
Go wild in the town,
The Goats of Llandudno
Because of lockdown.

Siân-Elin Flint-Freel

GREAT ORME GOAT MERCHANDISE GOES WORLDWIDE

S t David's Hospice, together with the rest of the planet, is living through extraordinary times. Back in March 2020, we had no choice but to close our twenty-six charity shops and two commercial cafés. We were forced to cancel our events and lottery cash collections. Even after the government's help, our worst fears were met when we estimated that we would face a shortfall of over £1 million by the end of the year.

We fought desperately to keep our inpatient service open throughout the pandemic, to be able to care for some of the most vulnerable people in our local communities living with a life-limiting illness. With social distancing restrictions, it was impossible to continue day therapy and this soon became an 'at home' service to ensure that patients' needs could be met.

In a bid to recover our losses during the first lockdown, we launched a £1 million 'Recovery Fund'. Almost immediately, support from the local community poured in as people and businesses came together to help.

The actions of the cheeky Great Orme Goats won't have escaped your attention during the first lockdown. After taking over the quiet streets of Llandudno in the absence of people, the goats soon became a viral sensation with videos and pictures being shared worldwide.

St David's Hospice is no stranger to these curious creatures, as they often wander down to our car park in early spring.

Thinking on our feet to find innovative ideas to help raise funds, we had the idea of the Great Orme goat charity tee shirt. Drawing upon the hospice's location on Abbey Road, we came up with a design which channelled The Beatles' iconic Abbey Road album cover – but instead featuring the goats trotting across the zebra crossing!

In the weeks following lockdown, national and worldwide press followed with two appearances on BBC Breakfast and further appearances on BBC Radio Wales, HENO, the Telegraph and Japanese news channel, TV Asahi.

We went global! Tee shirts have sold worldwide as far as Australia, America, Canada, Japan, China and across Europe.

Since its launch, the Great Orme Goat merchandise campaign has now sold over 9,000 tee shirts and 1,500 soft toys worldwide, bringing in a total income of over £350,000. Due to the generosity of the public, the hospice's £1 million pound recovery fund was met and the doors of the hospice remain firmly open for the people of North West Wales.

During the most challenging period the hospice has ever faced, we were able to keep our clinical colleagues on the front line by tapping into current affairs and ceasing an opportunity which was right in front of us – in the hospice car park.

The St David's Hospice Great Orme Goat products are available to purchase on the hospice website www. stdavidshospice.org.uk/shop. Each sale will contribute to the long-term recovery of the hospice, so that we are here in the future for local people who need our care. We are truly grateful for all the support we have received to date.

Margaret Hollings

St. David's Hospice

"We have enjoyed wonderful closeness and family time together."

LOCKDOWN LOWDOWN FROM 'THE MADHOUSE'

As the sole owner and director of the Anglesey Sea Zoo, I have lived on site at the business since I bought it 14 years ago. It's a stunning location with fields and the beach on my doorstep and a fantastic view over the Snowdonia mountains. I am a single mum and my family are far away, but my kids have grown up living here.

We love our crazy adventures and active family holidays and we're outdoors all year round – no such thing as bad weather, just the wrong kind of clothes!

When lockdown hit I still had animals to feed and care for and essential systems to maintain with running costs remaining high but no income from visitors. We were short of manpower and the boys mucked in with great delight – an extremely valuable education for them. The things they had enjoyed taking part in outside school hours were now essential work.

They trotted down to the beach with me to catch mysid, shrimps and crabs from the rockpools to feed our animals when we ran out of money to buy food in; they can now ID tricky species better than many Marine Biology graduates! They released juvenile common lobsters on the seashore, helped in caring for and releasing rescued seal pups and continued to keep our beach clean on our daily exercise. My eldest has become adept at taking videos for YouTube and these have captured our wonderful memories made from muddling through when thrown in at the deep end.

We have enjoyed wonderful closeness and family time together, although admittedly it has been more challenging than our usual frantic schedule fitted around schooldays and my long working hours.

The other household member has most definitely enjoyed our constant presence. I adopted Alfie, my batty Moluccan cockatoo, before I had the kids. She's a diva! She has self-harming issues and is as mad as a box of frogs but she's a real asset to the household and her moods make our day – from super cute chatting and entertaining, to stroppy and destructive. Although not helping with the workload, she more than makes up for it through evening entertainment when I am 'Zoomed Out'.

Alfie has had a presence in almost every online meeting, with her amazing knack of sitting quietly, good as gold until it is my turn to speak, then bouncing around squealing 'hello' and squawking for attention. As a result, my online meetings now start with "...and is it just you today, Frankie, or will the parrot be joining us again?"

It's been my toughest time ever since I bought the business, and it isn't over yet, but I am grateful to have my two little eco-warriors and 'the bird' to help me through it.

Frankie Hobro

Anglesey Sea Zoo

*"Lockdown gave me
a new life."*

HUSH

H ush said the world and we hushed. We slowed down, we listened. We saw each other again. Amid suffering and hearts bursting for those at risk, we had space to care, space for each other and space to think... like when the snow comes. An invisible blanket of snow lay all around the world. Noise lessened, time slowed... nature began to heal. Life began to heal.

But my hush began five years ago... sedately following the line of traffic forward, in the early dark, I gazed at my wonderful new husband, Steve. Christmas lights shining happily for us, journeying to buy our very first Christmas tree together.

It began with the loudest sound possible – a shocking explosion. A massive black BMW hooked right and smashed into us. Rammed across two lanes, searing the beacon off, rails contorting. Our car shot up and pounded back down. Our brand new married life was shattered before it'd begun. Succumbed to a wheelchair and walking aids, imprisonment in my own body was my life now. Learning minor tasks, I realised my vibrant life as a choreographer was over. We left to the Wales of shared family roots.

Our home was a tiny wooden hut, halfway down a verdant lane, nestled under the trees. The first impact was how green it was, then how still it was. No nervy city sounds. No traffic, planes – maybe the odd car, a chainsaw in the distance, birds. There'd be an owl at night, a scuffling badger.

Steve had to commute to London, but no matter how lovingly he parted, I felt left. The pace of life was screamingly slow... then luxuriously slow. But it was empty. Sorry – EMPTY!

Presently, the void became a quiet hush, something that healed... and there it was, in the stillness. Peace. I found peace.

Nature seeped into the cells of my broken body, my spirit. I could breathe. Our cottage was so humble, you could see the muddy ground between the old floor panels but it was home and we began to mend it. Then through local art classes, I found escape and hope.

So when the snow-like virus came, I was ready. All the lane, all the world, was together. Extraordinarily, for me, every single prolapsed disc retreated and injections were multiplied.

Suddenly, I could do more. I determined these months would be transformative. Breathing exercises, increased vitamins, physio for neck/spine injuries; I immersed myself in studying illustration, writing, becoming (gradually) more able. Each time Steve returned, he'd see change. By the end of Lockdown, I was strong enough for us to have a two-week holiday in Anglesey, where (incredibly) I met someone from a small publishing company. After interviewing artists from as far afield as the US, he asked me to become one of their featured illustrators!

I was blessed. Lockdown coincided with a key point in my treatment, giving me space to breathe and begin recovery. Never would I have dreamed it would lead to a career in illustration!

Lockdown gave me a new life.

Annette Aubrey-Bradshaw

SPONSORS AND PLEDGES

Thanks to our sponsors for making this Lockdown Legacy happen

Helping you to find the resources within, to overcome your barriers

 Qualified Person Centred Counsellor

 Business Coach

 Strength Based Trainer specialising in Neurodiversity

THE COACHING DEN
Motivational **Training & Mentorship 4 Life**

 TheCoachingDen4Life

 help@thecoachingden.co.uk

 07734 489953

 thecoachingden.co.uk

TINA OWEN FINANCIAL PLANNING LTD

An Associate Partner Practice of
St. James's Place Wealth Management

Our aim is to make financial advice available to all. We tailor our advice to each client's individual situation. You will hear us say:
"*We don't look after your money, we look after you!*"

01492 530000   tina.owen@sjpp.co.uk   www.tinaowenfp.co.uk
10 Carlton House, 68 Conway Road, Colwyn Bay, LL29 7LD

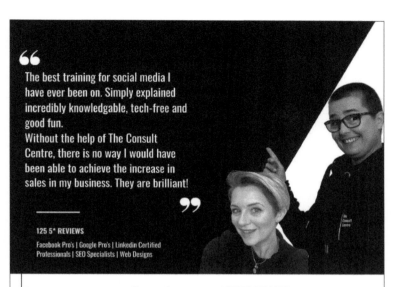

PLEDGES

- Active Background Checks
  www.activebackgroundchecks.com
- Angelic Healing
  www.angelicyou.co.uk
- Aphoria
  www.facebook.com/Aphoria-773227859487533/
- Bear Hunt Books
  www.bearhuntbooks.co.uk
- Blue Sky HR Consultancy
  www.blueskyhrconsultancy.co.uk
- Bryn Woodlands House
  www.brynwoodlandshouse.co.uk
- Debra Sima
- Freelance Performer, Director, Choreographer & Performing Arts Teacher
  www.twitter.com/Rastigger
- Glaslyn Artisan Ice Cream and Pizza
  www.glaslynices.co.uk
- Infinity CIC
  www.infinitycic.uk
- Jungle Goddess
  www.thejunglegoddess.com
- Kogan Coaching
  www.kogancoaching.com
- Leaf Organics
  www.leaforganics.uk

- **Looking Good Naturally**
  www.facebook.com/lookinggoodnaturallywithsandrapierce/
- **Louise Barson Art**
  www.louisebarson.co.uk
- **Morecambe Bay Wills & Estates Ltd**
  www.morecambebaywills.co.uk
- **No 1 Marketing Machine**
  www.no1marketingmachine.com
- **Peak Marquee Hire**
  www.peakmarqueehire.co.uk
- **Place 2 Print**
  www.place2print.co.uk
- **Sally Orange – endurance runner, adventurer & mental health champion**
  www.sallyorange.com
- **Sandra Smith**
- **STS North Wales**
  www.snowdoniasupplies.co.uk
- **Sunsets & Stars**
  www.facebook.com/sunsetsandstarsshepherdshut
- **Tacla Taid – The Anglesey Transport Museum & Cafe**
  www.angleseytransportmuseum.co.uk
- **The Cae Mor Hotel**
  www.caemorhotel.co.uk
- **The Consult Centre**
  www.theconsultcentre.com
- **The Happiness Well**
  www.facebook.com/TheHappinessWell
- **Utility Warehouse**
  www.mybillsfab.co.uk
- **Websprite**
  www.websprite.uk

CONTRIBUTORS

Alison Burleigh
Amanda Anderson
Amy Bennett
Angie Roberts
Ann Girling
Annette Aubrey-Bradshaw
Ava-Grace Needham
Beverley Bradley
Caroline Grant
Caroline Highman
Carolyn Eve
Catherine Sandland
Cerys Moore
Chris Kent
Christine Allen
Claire Evans
Deborah Twelves
Ella May Hastings
Elspeth Clark-Ellis
Emma Guy
Emma Wilson
Frankie Hobro
Ghazala Jabeen
Hyacinth Walters-Olsen
Iona Callaghan
Irene Wignall
Ivy Wood

Jill Bourne
Jo Mitchellhill
Jodie Murphy
Kalini Kent
Karen Williams OBE
Kat Massey
Kate Hardcastle MBE
Korena James
Larisa Bekresheva
Lauren Smith
Linda Davies
Lisa Bond
Lisa Haydn Davis
Louise Mackie
Lucy Monkman
Lymphoma Lass
Lyn Roseaman
Margaret Hollings
Marina Kogan
Mary Hennessey
Maura Jackson
Melissa Mackenzie
Michelle Kehoe
Michelle Louise
Moira Owen
Nicola Butler
Nicola Combe

Nicola Moore
Rachael Pierce Jones
Rachael Quinton
Rhian Hastings
Rob Stevens
Robyn Cain
Ruth Ballantine
Ruth Foulkes
Ruth Lloyd-Williams
Ruth Wilkinson
Sandra Smith
Sarah Elliott
Sarah Jarvis
Sarah Steinhöfel
Sheryl Viercant
Siân-Elin Flint-Freel

Sonia Goulding
Stephanie Billen
Sue Quinton
Sue Timperley
Suzy Bennett
Tamsin Hartley
Tansy Rogerson
Tatyana Leshkevich
Teresa Bushell
Teresa Carnall
Tracey Telford
Tracey Toulmin
Vicky Cutler
Wendy Stoneley
Yifan Nairn

9 781838 405014